STIRLING COUNCIL LIBRARIES

3804802 106519 3

D1143422

little

KEITH
LEMON

memoirs of
me Childhood

PARENTAL
ADVISORY
EXPLICIT CONTENT

CONTENTS

Little Keith Lemon

7

little keith lemon

This book is dedicated
to me mam, me brother,
and all the girls I've
mede love to. Oh, and
anyone who has bought me
a drink cos I'm on telly.
Love Keith x

A TWINKLE IN BILLY OCEAN'S EYE

If I'm honest, I can remember being a twinkle in me dad's eye. Just a twinkle. I'm not sure if he always had that twinkle in his eye but I knew he had his eye on me mam. I started out in life as a one-nightstand. Thirty years ago, me mam was at one of Billy Ocean's gigs. I fink she had won tickets for a Radio 1 roadshow where he were playing and that is how it all began. I fink it were in Leeds, near Yorkshire telly. Billy, me dad, were kind of like the Russell Brand of his day, except he were black, he din't have long hair and he din't wear girls' jeans. Not that there is anything wrong with wearing girls' jeans. I fink he looks right cool, Russell, I just don't have the gumption to wear girls' jeans. Every time I'd have to go for a wee and I have to do the buttons up the wrong way, I would get confused. Anywhere, Billy Ocean were like the Russell Brand of his day – a master of the art of seduction. Me mam has always said he were a right gentleman and very friendly. He spotted her in the crowd and asked her if she wanted to go backstage. He were so friendly that he let her play with his tallywhacker in his dressing room and you know the rest. I don't know if it is 100% true or not because I have never been on *Jeremy Kyle* and had a DMA test. But I have met him and we did have an

He were like the Russell
Brand of his day...

instant bond. There was a real connection between us, like father like son. Both thick as a Coke can.

It's never really bothered me that I were the product of a one-nightstand. I fink me mam were worried about it but I got Billy Ocean as me dad! *Sha-ting!* Being a feminist, I've always thought it were unfair that if you were a man and you have a lot of one–nightstands, you get called a stud whereas if you ware a woman having one–nightstands, people fink you're a dirty slapper. But there's nowt wrong with being a dirty slapper. Dirty slappers have a lot more fun and as time goes on I'm sure that the stigma of being one is being eradicated around the world. Perhaps I should start a charity which brecks down the stigma around dirty slappers, it is somet I could really put me heart and soul into.

MEETING DAD -
TWO HALVES
OF ONE WHOLE

Anywhere, it were only two years ago when I met me
dad properly. I din't see me dad when I were growing
up. I only saw him on telly, on *Top of t'Pops*. That's
why I used to love *Top of t'Pops* so much, it's the only
time I would get to see me dad. When I were really
young, I din't even know it were me dad but I just felt
a real connection with him. Me mam confessed to me
when I were about nine. She just came out and said it,
'I fink Billy Ocean could be your dad'. 'What? Me dad's
black? How come I'm not black?' But she explained
that sometimes it skips a generation. You know, like,
ginger hair. Or in *Teen Wolf* where his dad's a wolf, and
Teen Wolf is one – but he might not have been if it had
skipped him. But it din't. Know what I'm saying? Good,
I'll commence.

It were a strange experience coming face to face with
me father. He were right nice and agreed to be in me
film, which by the way did really well! £2.1 million to
meck it and mede over £10.5 million. So, critics can go
eat my arse! Oooosh! Anyway . . . He knew that I had

been going around revealing that he were me dad and I know to many people they thought it were a ludicrous idea, but he knew there were somet in it. Like I said, we had an instant connection and we both just knew. Even with his daughters. I knew we were related somehow as I didn't want to shag them I just wanted to hug 'em and say 'I love you, sister. I wish we could have been closer. You are the black sister I knew I had but never had but always wanted.' When we really discussed it, we just cried for two hours. He said that he din't really want to get with me mam because he doesn't really know her properly. In the 80s, he was a naughty lad, but everyone was back then. I wonder how many half brothers and sisters I have dotted around the world! He said, 'let's just continue how we are and we'll see each other every now and then.' He did a gig in the Epcot Centre in Disney recently and I went to see him. He did a shout out to me. Boy has he still got some moves. Must be where I got me rhythm from because it ain't from me mam! The fans were mental for him. It were nice to see he had so much love from people. I just kept finking, 'that's me dad up there!' Fucking 'ell!

THE HEAD OF THE HOUSEHOLD, ME MAM

Me mam is a wonderful woman. She has got two arms, two legs and strawberry blonde hair. Her's is out of a bottle because I remember her wearing one of those funny caps . . . I either have images of me mam looking beautiful or images of me mam with that rubber johnny with holes in with hair coming through. She's a Leeds girl through and through. She were brought up there and would never leave. As Billy was out and about touring, and I don't fink he even knew about me until recently, me mam brought me and our Greg up by herself. I remember when me mam and me found out for sure that our Greg was a willy smoker. We were both together at the time and we came home and caught Greg in the kitchen with another fella with a mouthful. So he got caught out rather than actually coming out. He said he weren't sure if he definitely were gay or not but I told him, 'Greg, cock in mouth, it means you are. You are hormone.' I fink it were quite a weight off his shoulders to have it out there, although it were a bit of a shock for me mam, especially walking in on them like that! I fink she did struggle with our Greg's sexuality at first. I fink she thought she could come up with a cure for it with the right mixture of Calpol and Lemsips. She'd not come across many gays because she's from a different time when people were less open about these things, but Greg and I have educated her about homosexuality, saying, just because he is a willy smoker, it doesn't make him a bad

person. Our Greg is the nicer one out of the two of us. If we're at a party he'll befriend everyone before I do. I'm more stubborn, you see. He'll go out of his way to be nice. But since that day we came home and found him smoking sausage, he has been happierer ever since, so that is all me mam ever wanted.

Everyfing me mam did was for us. I fink me mam is a bit like me, or I'm a bit like me mam. She does fings to make people laugh and start a conversation. It's like the bandage I wear on me hand. I've been wearing that ever since I were seventeen and me mate still says to me 'Your hand can't still be brocken.' But the dingbat is missing the point. It mekes me look like I'm a man about town. I look like I've had adventures. It is a good ice brecker and it starts conversations. I've said it before and I'll say it again, it's a minge magnet, let me tell you.

'Ooo look at that wounded soldier, he's probably been in the Navy.' 'What do you do in the Navy?' 'I do ship fings and stuff.' It depicts that you are an adventurous man, a thrillseeker. A real man's man, like David Hasselhoff.

Me mam is the same. She is really good at socialising and not afraid to elaborate on the facts to make a good story. Even though we can both be dingbats, other people seem to like us as we are fun and we have the banter. Me mam is getting on a bit now of course and she reminds me of the stupid one out of *Golden Girls*. But I mean that with all niceness. She is just a bit ditzy. She burns toast every time she cooks it. But she's always been a bit of a ropey cook. I once got food poisoning from a sausage roll and baked beans that she made me. I was shitting constantly for two days. I nearly fainted.

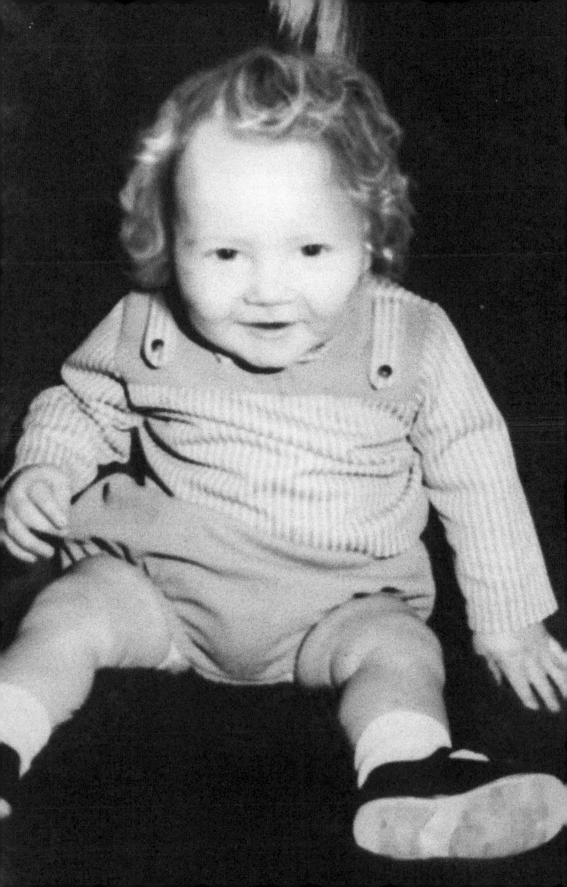

OUR GREG!

The final member of our family unit is our Greg who I've just mentioned. I remember when our Greg were born, I were seven years old and I were dead excited to have a little brother to play with. I've always been a little bit in a world of me own, so I didn't compete for attention too much and it were nice talking to someone else other than me mam. Up until that point, it had been just me and me mam so it did feel strange to have someone else, but there were enough of an age difference so it weren't like we were always wanting to get off with the same girl or anything. Turns out, I needn't have worried about that in any case as he is a hormonesexual. I've always thought it must have been hard for me mam. She had one really good-looking son, me, and one not so good-looking one as he were, you know, less physically blessed with aesthetics.

Gregory was always a lot quieterer than me, but he weren't shy. He just din't grab fings by the balls like I always did. I'll rephrase that, cos he did actually grab balls but not till he was older. But what I meant were that he din't put himself out there, if you know what I mean. He's different now. He chats to everyone, but he's not like me.

We never really looked alike as I was better looking and still am, but you could always tell we were related. We both had the same strawberry blond hair and cheeky smile. He never had as good a dress sense as me, he's a bit conservative. A bit preppy like. I looked out for him a lot when he was a kid. T'other kids cun't understand why he played with girls' toys. I cun't either really, but that din't mean there were owt wrong with him or he was a bad kid. Sometimes I envied him as he had a lot of girl mates. In fact, sometimes that was handy cos there were always girls hanging around the place. When we were a bit older, we had similar taste in birds. He always liked the fit ones like Kylie and Belinda Carlisle and stuff, but he wanted to be them, whilst I wanted to be in them!

I fink Greg used to look up to me as a kid cos I always knew how t'enjoy meself, whereas he was always quite sensible. It isn't till he's come out that he's really started enjoying himself and I'm right happy for him. I mean, don't get me wrong, I've walked in on him whilst he's been enjoying himself too much and I wasn't too happy about seeing that. Not pecifically cos he's a sausage smoker, it's nowt t'do with that. It's just embarrassing in't it? If he was a sister and I caught her with a mouthful of cock that'd be embarrassing too.

We don't talk about Greg's dad as he is in prison, but as neither of us had a dad around it din't really make much difference. We were a little band of three. I fink that is partly why I was quite mature. I had to be. I were the man about the house and me mam needed me to look after fings for her.

OUR [HOUSE] AND AUNTIE JEAN'S

Greg and I were both born in Leeds General Infirmary.
But soon after I were born, me mam brought me back
to our house – the same house that we lived in all the
time me and Greg were growing up. It were in a little
close with about ten other houses. In me head it was
like an American sitcom with white picket fences
and lots of beautiful children laughing in the streets.
And there was a cool guy in a leather jacket that said
'Heeey' a lot. Oh no, that's the Fonze from *Happy Days*.
In reality, it were a little bit different. Me Auntie, Jean,
she lived in one of t'other houses at the end of the close
and she were always popping round. There were a lad
the same age as me who lived in one of the houses
opposite, he were called Tommy Bell and he were me
first friend. We spent a lot of time together when we
were younger, we were proper best mates and we'd
always be at one another's doing somet or other.
Years later, it were Belly who used to write the rude
words behind the door in the wardrobe that me mam

WANK

TODGER TALLY WACKER

DICK

FANNY

KEITH
WOZ
ERE

got so angry about when she found them. He were clever and wrote my name so that me mam thought it were me. He were right cheeky but, like me, he had that ability to charm the ladies and me mam used to fink the sun shined out of his arse. She wouldn't have been so charmed if she'd known that he'd just drawn some bangers on the wardrobe with a compass. Proper round bangers!

Anywhere, looking back now, I can see it were a bit rough where we lived, but when ya know all't roughuns it don't feel that rough t'you. There was always a mattress outside on't road for some reason. You don't see that in American sitcoms, do ya? And it were always very exciting when a burnt-out car appeared in't street. It weren't a big house but it wasn't a small 'un either. Me and Greg always had separate bedrooms, so that was cool. I remember when we were kids we use t'get the mattress off t'bed and slide down t'steps on it. It sounds like I was obsessed with mattresses, don't it? Yeah, we'd have fights like any other brother and sister. Just play fights like that got outta hand. Once I kicked our Greg in't balls and he had t'go t'hospital cos it went up inside him. I felt really bad. Ya should never kick someone in't balls. The pain is incredible. Like a reverse orgasm.

Me mam and our Greg still live there in that same house. Our kid worships me mam, as do I, but he still hasn't left home. He still lives with me mam in that close! He's got a fella but I expect he'll move in to me mam's before our Greg moves out. It's good that mam is very liberal. When we were kids he stuck t'her like glue. Don't get me wrong, I worship me mam, but I just needed less guidance cos I've always been quite mature. I know what I wanna do and where I wanna go.

Our kid does too, he wants t'go in't arse – ha, ha, ha, ha. I'm kidding. He don't actually do that though, he's told me. Him and his fella just suck and toss. Not sure he'll appreciate me telling ya like. Anywhere, it's a nice comforting feeling knowing that our kid is there t'look after me mam whilst I'm down in't big smoke.

It were a nice place to grow up, that close. One of the best things was that our garden backed onto the local girls' school so when we were a bit older, Tommy and I used to sit in the garden encouraging the girls while they were running around doing cross country. In pants! They used to make them run around in pants! They wun't do that now, would they?

ME FIRST WORDS

Anywhere, other than being a twinkle in Billy's eye, I don't really remember much before I was about five. I don't fink your brain starts working until you're five, does it? Me mam always likes to remind me that me first words were biscuit and minge. I'm proud of that. Good to see I had me priorities straight from a young age.

But when I was a kid your minge wasn't a word you used to refer to a lady's love hole, yer minge was yer face. You'd say, 'Ooo, look at t'minge on him!' This would be the kind of conversation me and me mam would have:

Me mam: What's up with you?
Me: Nowt!
Me mam: Have you been fighting with him again?
Me: Yeah, our Greg's put a dress on me Action Man. There's summat wrong with our Greg!
Me mam: Cheer up! Look at t'minge on him! Look at t'minge on our Keith!

I remember the moment when minge turned, in my brain, to being a rude word. I couldn't believe me mam had been touting it around the kitchen saying 'look at me minge!' I don't suppose she knew but at the same, it's not right is it?! Yer minge was yer face. Yer mouth was part of yer minge. 'Mam, I want a biscuit for me minge'. That was the sentence I were working towards when I learnt me first two words.

I tell yer what term or word I never use to describe a ladyhole: Beaver. I hated it when me kids book,

The Beaver and the Elephant, was announced and everyone thought I was referring to a lady's minge. It's a kid's book, why would I be chatting about minges? It's out now by the way. Get it for your kids, they'll love it! Cha-mone motha plugga!

I didn't start properly talking till I were about four. But I am making up for it now. I just pointed at stuff and would go 'ugh', 'biscuit', 'minge'. And then it just came one day, almost overnight, and I couldn't stop meself.

I were obsessed with Bourbon biscuits so I had to
work out a way to get me hands on some of those.
When I was a little bit older, I used to play out with
me mates, and I can remember pretending to be Bob
Geldof, saying 'do you all want some biscuits? I'm
gonna get you some.' And then I'd go into our house,
go t'biscuit tin and have a rummage in the bread bin,
and I'd put loads of biscuits in between slices of thick
white bread and make biscuit sandwiches. 'Just getting
a piece of bread, Mam' because I weren't allowed to
have biscuits, but I were allowed bread so if me mam
caught me on the way out, she'd fink I were just having
a piece of bread. And then I'd dish the biscuits out to
me mates. I were a bit like the Milky Bar Kid but with
biscuits. The biscuits are on me! I were a biscuit dealer
and it made me feel like a hero like Robert De Niro.
That's a line from a Finlay Quaye song. You don't
hear owt from him any more do ya? I wonder what he
is up to. You know Zammo from *Grange Hill* works as
a key cutter? Well I'm not sure if he still does but I saw
him at a key cutters in Soho a while back. Crazy times.
I hope that don't happen to me. Not that key cutting
is a bad fing. We need key cutters! But I don't fink
it would be me cuppa tea. I'm not good with me
hands – unless I'm with a lass, d'ya get me? Yeah boi!

DREAMS OF BEING A SPACEMAN, AN ICE-CREAM-VAN MAN, AND RICHARD BRANSON

I couldn't wait to get to school. At home, it were just me and me mam, as our Greg hadn't popped out yet, so I were looking forward to testing out me new words and making some more friends. Obviously, I knew Tommy already as our mams used to put us both in our prams at the front of our houses to watch the world go by. Tommy were on one side of t'road and I were on t'other. Our mams used to spend hours talking over the fence at each other.

I remember me first day – running up to the gates of St Michael's like I were going to a theme park or summat. The first day at school weren't as intimidating as it might have been as I already knew Tommy, so that was cool. I fink it were a friendship of convenience at first but once I got used to having him around, he were like the brother I never had. Not that our Greg weren't a proper brother but he were more

little keith lemon

Barbie than Action Man and he weren't around for
the first seven years anyway.

I can remember making friends with everyone straight
away. I liked school and didn't have any of those days
where you don't want to go and you're crying and
clinging on to your mam's leg begging not to go in.
When I got there I liked it cos I'd learnt to talk and
I liked talking. It felt like school was miles away but
it was just up t'road. Everything seems so far when
you are a kid, don't it? In fact, I remember when we
went camping with cubs, it felt like we were miles
away and we were actually just on t'other side of the
girls' school that I could see from me house.

But while I liked school, I don't fink I were one of the
most academically gifted kids in me class. I din't need
to be. I could talk me way in and out of most situations
so it din't really matter whether a piece of paper said
I were good at somet or not. When I were young
I wanted to be a spaceman, an ice-cream-van man
and Richard Branson. All at once. On his day off, the
spaceman would sell ice cream at a lower cost to
disadvantaged kids who can't afford to buy a 99 with
a Flake. Even back then I understood that the ladies
love it if they fink you go all soft over a few
disadvantaged kids. The idea of being on telly din't
properly enter me head until I were a fully grown adult.
I had a trip to London and thought, yeah, I'd like to live
there. It looks exciting. And when I came to London it
was exciting. But it weren't a dream of mine when I was
a kid, even though me mam said that I always wanted
to be famous, but not a famous TV presenter, I just
wanted to be known. I wanted to be known for somet,
but I din't know it were telly. When I was thirteen, I just
wanted to be known for having the biggest willy, but it

little keith lemon

were right small . . . Was it fuck! It were massive!
Like a straight cumberland sausage.

Come to fink of it, Richard Branson is another
candidate for being me dad – I've been told I look
like him. Can't fink why as I clearly look more
like Billy Ocean than Richard Branson. Look:

DAD?

DAD?

But I guess it were his entrepreneurial spirit
that I admired. I wanted to be an international
businessman like Branson. I've met him more
recently – I fink we admire each other's work.
Me mam just wanted me to not be a thief or
a drug-taker, really. The main fing that mattered
to me mam was that our Greg and I were happy.
I fink she's glad that I turned out to be the man
that I am today.

TO OPEN, → PULL HERE

My favourite subject at school was swimming.
It weren't a posh school so we din't have a swimming
pool at the school or owt, so we'd all get on a bus they'd
hired instead. It were a bus bus, not like a school bus,
a proper bus, like in London they're red, in Leeds they
were green. They'd have one of them to pick us up to
take us to the swimming baths and I don't know how
many weeks we'd been going but one day I noticed
there were a big red lever on the wall of the bus, near
the window, and it said: TO OPEN, PULL HERE.
I thought, 'right, I'll pull it then.' Whoo whoo whoo.
It were like the whole bus were an alarm and it started
going off. The bus stopped and we could all hear the
driver huffin' and puffin'. And then the teacher,
Ms Mumphries, came upstairs: 'Who opened the fire
door?' Well I din't know it was for fire. It just said,
TO OPEN, PULL HERE and then there were this big
red lever. It were the back window all along the back of
the bus. I just opened it. I fink she could tell by the
look in me eye that it were me. So she made a big show
of laying down the rules but I knew she were gonna let
me off. She always had a bit of a soft spot for me.

Every time I was on a bus after that it came over me
like a wave that I wanted to pull that red lever and
open t'fire door but because I knew it was a fire door
I din't. I couldn't go swimming for two weeks because
I opened the fire door which meant two weeks of not
looking at lasses in swimming costumes and also

meant everyone was gonna become more advanced.
I had an image in me mind that they were all gonna
be like *Man From Atlantis* by the time I went back and
I was gonna be like some bellend that can't swim with
fucking armbands! Armbands! Two weeks is a long
time when you're a kid. Anyfing could happen!

I did get me bronze eventually but it took me a while
to catch up. I had to swim 400m which took ages and
I thought 'I'm gonna die here. Anything I have to do
after this I'm gonna be too fucked to do.' And then
I had to save a brick in me pyjamas. I can remember

little keith lemon

finking, 'I don't understand this concept. So the brick represents a person that I'm saving that's drowning but I can only save them if I'm wearing pyjamas? So what if I'm walking past a river and someone is in there drowning but I don't have any pyjamas on me? Do I leave 'em? Do I run home and go get me pyjamas and go, 'right, now I'll save you because I've got me pyjamas on?'

Anywhere, I was really chuffed about having me sew-on bronze swimming badge. I'd sew the badges on me trunks but you got a little enamel badge in a red plastic case as well and you know what I thought when I got that? You can fuck all your other awards, all I wanted were that badge and I din't give a shit anymore. So the next year, when I had to do me silver, I cheated. I can remember t'bit where you're doing your metres, it looked like I were swimming but I were actually just walking along the bottom. You know when you get t'shallow end? Just walking. And every time I saw the teacher I'd lift me legs up. I got another badge but I din't care because I had me bronze. Forget silver, gold and lifesaving. But it was weird that kids the same age were doing their lifesaving whilst I were doing bronze. They were saving lives and I were saving some bricks in me pyjamas. Oh shit, that foam brick looks like it's in trouble! Better get me pyjamas on.

It set me up for the future though. When we were a bit older, me mate Talbot and I used to go to t'swimming baths on a Sunday. Oh it was disappointing if you forgot your goggles. We weren't actually there to swim. We just looked at girls. We din't even try and chat 'em up. We'd just jump in, get a right good look at t'girls under t'water and then come up out of the water like we were in *Apocalypse Now*. We'd just look at each other.

I don't even fink we said anything. We just smiled at each other, knowing. All that swimming gave me a few ideas for the future. A splash about in the swimming baths is one of my favourite first date ideas – I can show off my athletic ability and Olympic body whilst swimming to collect a brick. The only difference between then and now is that then I wore me pyjamas but now I just swim naked. It's like getting an advanced review in't it? You can have a good look and go, 'yeah, that'll do for me'. Otherwise you might fall head over heels for someone, get them back to your house, get naked and find out that she has a weird lump on her back that has a toenail on the end of it. From the front she's great but from behind I'm gonna see that toenail looking at me all the time. Do I ask, 'have you got a toenail growing on your back?'

Kylie is so fit it hurts. I would have liked to take her swimming and give her some TLC – Tender Lemon Cuddles

You learn a lot more about someone by treating her to a trip down t'baths than you would at the cinema. It's weird going to the cinema with someone, innit? A quintessential date, the cinema, but really you should go to the cinema with your mates or by yourself, not with a date. If you are going to go to the cinema on a date, make it a horror film. When she gets scared of the bogey man, you can slip your arm around her and play the gent. Then offer her some of your popcorn which you have previously put your tallywhacker in (you can cut a hole out the bottom) – she'll grab a right handful. Oooosh! Getting a handjob in't cinema . . . Living the dream!

Anywhere, Talbot and I also used to dare each other to dive off the diving board. I never did it. In fact, I only dived off top diving board when I was doing *Celebrity Juice* and it was Keith versus Jedward. Well, I didn't actually dive, I jumped, but I can remember finking, I'm not having those little bastards beat me at this. I didn't look down. I just walked straight off and then watched them go, 'oh, we can't do it, we can't do it, we can't do it.' The dingbats! Nice kids though.

little keith lemon

THE FAMOUS ~~FIVE~~ 4

Anywhere, back to St Michael's. Tommy and I met
Dave Fletcher and Frank Pistle at school. We were
like the Famous Five, only there were four of us and
we weren't all gonna be famous. Obviously we din't
know that back then but I were always a bit of a
performer. Tommy became known as Belly as he
had a bit of timber on him and his surname was Bell.
Simple as peas. As I said, I'd known Belly all me life
– even before we went to primary school – so we were
like brothers really. Belly was a nice guy, bit strange,
but a nice guy underneath it all. He still is! Nice but
a bit strange. Because he lived over t'road from us,
he would come over all the time. When we were older,
I fink he were a bit intrigued by hormonesexuals
so he came just to have a look at our Greg. He were
completely bamboozled that he was playing with girls'
toys as we played with Action Men and cars behind
sofa. Once Belly and I both fell asleep behind the sofa
and when me mam couldn't find us she thought that
we'd been kidnapped or somet. She went out in t'street
looking for us both. In't that weird, we were playing so
hard with our cars we actually fell asleep? But because
me mam thought we'd been nicked she called the
police! I can remember just waking up behind t'sofa,
both of us, rubbing our eyes and finking 'eh, what's
going on? Why is me mam talking to a copper?'
We knew that summat were going on. She weren't
best pleased when we crept out from behind the
sofa rubbing our sleepy eyes.

Frank Pistle's nickname were Pisshole. We used to tease him whenever he met a bird and say we gave him that name because he used to piss himself in class all the time, but it were really just because he had a daft name. Dave was just Dave. We were all in the same class and all sat on the back row of desks, apart from Belly who had to sit close to teacher cos he had a squiffy eye. We just used to mess around all t'time, passing notes to each other. We were never that naughty, just the right side of cheeky. If I ever started getting into trouble I would just tell the teacher how much I wanted to learn but how difficult I found it and how frustrating it were that I couldn't keep up with everyone else. It seemed to do the trick.

Hey Daz mate. Apparently you're got a scout walker for sale. I'll give you £1.50 for it.
Keith

Are you having a laugh? It was about £8 quid. £6?
Daz

Go stick nettles up ya arse, I'll give you £2.50
£5.50
I'll swap you it for skeletor?

Yeah nice one

Cool, I'll bring it in tomorrow.

Ha ha, what a dingbat! Skeletor cost less than a scout walker. I was always good at swapping shit. I once swapped a Panini sticker book for a BMX. It was a rubbish BMX, but still a bike for some stickers. I had business acumen at the age of seven!

MY FIRST CRUSH

I fancied girls before anyone started fancying girls
in my class. When I first started primary school, I can
remember fancying this girl called Penny and I were
only about six. I'd fink about her all the time. I would
chase her round the playground and then I would just
ignore her when I actually got close enough to talk
to her. When you're a kid you don't know what your
emotions are and you can't deal with them, can you?
I'd chase her, then ignore her, then chase her again.
But I actually wanted to kiss her, but I didn't know what
kissing was. I remember feeling very strange around
her and then when she left school to go and live in
America, I can remember being slightly sad but I couldn't
tell anyone because I didn't know what I was feeling.

I soon got back on the horse as she had a couple of fit
mates. I can't remember their names, mind. I tell you
what though, finking about it, her sister was fit as well.
Again, older. Her sister must have been about three
years older and I remember finking, bloody hell,
she's like a fitter version of her. Once some disabled
children came to our school to prove that kids with
disabilities can still play musical instruments, and
one of the girls that were playing the harp looked
almost exactly like Penny's sister. I can remember
finking, right, this is my chance, I might be able to
pull her. But I didn't because I thought it would be
an awkward relationship. I tell you what, all credit to
people who go out with people who have disabilities.
They're good people them. Unless they're just using
them for their disabled parking badge.

Anywhere, at that age we spent a lot of time trying
to work out whether we disliked or if we liked girls.
It were dead confusing. I remember Dave had a tree
in his garden that we used to climb as he fancied his
next-door neighbour and it gave us a right good view
into her bedroom. It were a couple of years later that
we found out that it were his cousin! Dirty bastard had
been spying on his cousin all that time. I remember
saying to him, 'you can't fancy your cousin!' And he'd
go, 'yeah, but she ain't really me cousin.' But she were.
Dirty Dave fancied his cousin. Dirty Bastard!

To be fair to him, she was right fit. She used to wave at us sometimes. Little tease. She were a nice girl, Emma Bunton girl-next-door kind of pretty. You know, with that little rabbit-nose thing going on. But we were getting to that age where boys become boys and girls become girls and we went through that stage where you hate girls, don't you? And girls hate boys. But you kind of love them at the same time. It's all a bit confusing. It might be overnight that you suddenly start liking them again and before you know it you've got your tongue in their mouth and you're cleaning the windows.

Dave's cousin had a little rabbit nose like that. Dead cute.

Michelle Keegan reminds me of Dave's sister Beth. F.A.F.

I could see why Dirty Dave fancied his cousin but I was more interested in his sister, Beth. She was Fit As Flip. If I had to compare her to anyone now it would be Michelle Keegan. She is one of me all-time favourites is Michelle. I would destroy her. We've had her on *Juice* a few times now and she drank a pint of lager that had some jizm in it. What a great lass. Good luck to her and Mark Wright. He's a good lad, too. But he wears his clobber too tight – it looks like it's hurting him.

DRESSING UP AND PLAYING THE  HERO

Anywhere, I always wanted to hang out with Beth and hear what she and her friends were saying and stuff. I can actually remember when it was Beth's birthday and both me and Dave came down and ruined the birthday because we were both dressed as superheroes and stole her thunder. I was dressed as Spiderman and he was dressed as The Hulk and he ripped all his pyjamas up. He wasn't green, though, he just ripped his pyjamas and I fink all his sister's mates thought we were really cute and funny. We were jumping around finking we were superheroes and then he got done by his mam for ripping his pyjamas up and for stealing the attention away from Beth.

I remember that day very clearly as I remember it were the first time I thought that a girl was extraordinarily fit ... but at the same time I knew I wasn't old enough to properly like girls. She made me tingle in areas that I din't know were supposed to tingle. She had this long super-straight brown hair and she used to flick it around like they do in't films. It has always been like that for me though. I've been advanced when it comes to women. I din't start writing poetry for girls until a little later but she did inspire me to put pen to paper. I was only eight at the time but with a few drawings I usually had 'em wrapped round my little finger.

Beth, if you're out there, give us a call. Dave's got me number. We could go swimming together and I'll treat you to Nando's after.

I always knew I'd look cute when I dressed up. I was in t'cubs when I were younger as I knew I'd look cute in the uniform. I don't remember much about cubs except being in a tent in the wood round the corner from where we lived. Belly were there too. I had toothache so I put a Wine Gum in me tooth to act as a filling. I thought I were being really clever. That'll sort it out. That'd fill it. But the week after I had to have me whole tooth yanked out!

I did graduate to scouts but it were shit and I said to Belly, 'watch me, I'm gonna run out'. He said, 'no you're not.' I said, 'I am. I'm gonna grab me Michael Jackson Thriller jacket and I'm gonna run out.' And I did, I just ran for it. And that were the end of me scouting career.

In me mind she looks like this, like a little Pocahontas. I'd poke her hontas.

Me in modern day times.
I got this costume from a
Japanese website for $65.
I wore it at Comic-Con -
I looked ace amongst 300
other spidermen sweating
their tits off in the San Diego heat.

Date: No:

Beth asked me what me new years resolutions are. I had to make some up on t'spot to impress her. Going to try and stick to 'em.

① STOP SWEARING. A few weeks ago, I watched a programme and it were called John's Not Mad. It were about something called tourettes and John used to say things he shouldn't say all the time. I almost wished I had tourettes because it would have given me an excuse but me mam is always banging on at me about swearing and she said she wouldn't buy us any more bourbons until I stop swearing.

② STOP CLIMBING OUT OF ME BEDROOM WINDOW WITH TOMMY AT 1 AM. Last time we did it, Tommy broke his arm and had a cast and all the fit girls signed it. But now he says it is starting to itch and it is really smelly so it weren't worth it.

③ GET A SUPER FIT GIRLFRIEND and smooch for three minutes, no stopping.

DEE

I went out with a girl when I was nine; that was probably my first relationship. I mean it weren't a serious one – I was nine and she was nine. Her name was Dee and she was in my class at school. She was a pretty girl-next-door kind of girl with long blonde hair and she were a bit taller than me. She reminded me of a girl that used to be in *Baywatch*, I can't remember her name, but she was also in *ET* as a child. And I don't mean Drew Barrymore.

I went out with her for about six weeks. That's basically six years in grown-up terms. As we were both infants we didn't have any sexual exploits but there was a lot of kissing. Another friend would time us kissing to see how long we could last. I don't know why we were timed because we weren't gonna try and get in t'*Guinness Book of Records* or anything, but we could say to our

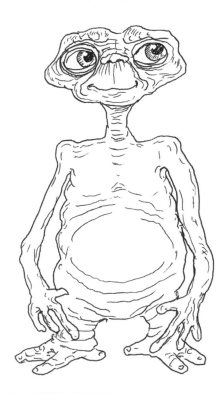

Keith
A
Dee

friends that we kissed for two minutes. Just smooching for two whole minutes! Can you imagine smooching that long now? Smooching and nothing else. There wasn't any tongue action. We din't really go on dates or owt, we just used to hang out after school. We went out for the school holidays and then six weeks after it all began, it ended. The summer of love. She went and did somet that only a right dingbat would ever do: she cut her long, super-straight hairs short and permed the whole lot. I said, 'it looks like you've got a wig on! What have you done to your barnet? We're over.' It were over. She looked like Kevin Webster from *Corrie* in 1989!

It were that same summer that we went on a family holiday to Rhyl – perhaps that put a strain on our relationship. She must have felt like I abandoned her so went and chopped all her hairs off. As a family we din't have enough money to go abroad but we did go on holidays by the sea. We went to Rhyl, Scarborough and Blackpool. Rhyl was me favourite – I even had a T-shirt saying, 'Keeping it Rhyl'. I've always been at the front edges of fashion.

The highlights of the holiday were always the same: fishing and eating hot doughnuts. I fink it used to cost a pound for about 136 doughnuts. You got such a huge bag of doughnuts for a quid. We'd be eating doughnuts all day. We'd go in t'sea back then because you didn't know it was full of shit. But you don't go in t'sea now in England, do you, because you just fink it's gonna be turds floating past you, don't you?

little keith lemon

THE GRATTAN'S CATALOGUE'S ARRIVED. CHRISTMAS IS COMING!

When I were growing up, my favourite time of the year were Christmas. Not actually Christmas itself, but the build up to it. The first sign of Christmas for me weren't the Coca-Cola advert or the Christmas songs that would be playing in Woolworths from September, it was the Grattan's catalogue coming through t'door. We'd get a catalogue as thick as Yellow Pages through t'door and I were like, 'oooo it's Christmas soon, innit?' Me and Gregory would just sit there with the catalogue on our lap going, 'want that, want this . . . ' It was the way you would write down your Christmas list – 'want that, want that, want that, want that'. You din't circle them or anyfing, you weren't allowed to draw in it – you'd get into trouble with mam if you did that. Once we were done with writing up our imaginary Christmas lists, I would turn to the underwear pages. Obviously Greg were less interested in the underwear section and always used to look at the curling tongs and such. I had some romantic nights with that Grattan's catalogue, I did. When me mam were out and our kid was in bed I'd wank over it on t'bra pages.

little keith lemon

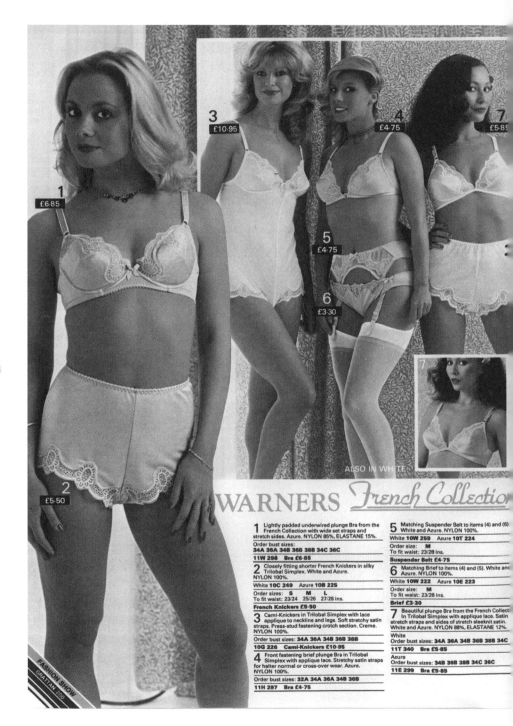

1 £6·85

3 £10·95

4 £4·75

7 £5·85

5 £4·75

6 £3·30

2 £5·50

7

ALSO IN WHITE

FASHION SHOW
GRATTAN 200

WARNERS *French Collectio*

1 Lightly padded underwired plunge Bra from the French Collection with wide set straps and stretch sides. Azure. NYLON 85%, ELASTANE 15%.
Order bust sizes:
34A 36A 34B 36B 38B 34C 36C
11W 298   Bra £6·85

2 Closely fitting shorter French Knickers in silky Trilobal Simplex. White and Azure. NYLON 100%.
White **10C 249**   Azure **10B 225**
Order sizes: S   M   L
To fit waist: 23/24   25/26   27/28 ins.
French Knickers £5·50

3 Cami-Knickers in Trilobal Simplex with lace applique to neckline and legs. Soft stretchy satin straps. Press-stud fastening crotch section. Creme. NYLON 100%.
Order bust sizes: 34A 36A 34B 36B 38B
10G 226   Cami-Knickers £10·95

4 Front fastening brief plunge Bra in Trilobal Simplex with applique lace. Stretchy satin straps for halter normal or cross-over wear. Azure. NYLON 100%.
Order bust sizes: 32A 34A 36A 34B 36B
11H 297   Bra £4·75

5 Matching Suspender Belt to items (4) and (6) White and Azure. NYLON 100%.
White **10W 259**   Azure **10T 224**
Order size: **M**
To fit waist: 23/28 ins.
Suspender Belt £4·75

6 Matching Brief to items (4) and (5). White and Azure. NYLON 100%.
White **10W 222**   Azure **10E 223**
Order size: **M**
To fit waist: 23/28 ins.
Brief £3·30

7 Beautiful plunge Bra from the French Collecti In Trilobal Simplex with applique lace. Satin stretch straps and sides of stretch sleeknit satin. White and Azure. NYLON 88%, ELASTANE 12%.
White
Order bust sizes: 34A 36A 34B 36B 38B 34C
11T 340   Bra £5·85
Azure
Order bust sizes: 34B 36B 38B 34C 36C
11E 299   Bra £5·85

SUPER BANG!

5
£4·99

9
£5·99

10
£7·99

6
£5·50

7
£14·99

8
£3·75

'Moonlighter' by Julie Anne. Underwired glamour Bra with slightly padded undercup and stretch wing panels. Lingerie soft stretch straps. Purple/Black or Red/Black NYLON 83%, POLYESTER 12%, ELASTANE 5%.

Purple/Black 11C 206   Red/Black 11W 306
Order bust sizes:
34A 36A 34B 36B 38B 34C 36C 38C
Price £4·99

'Moonlighter' matching Brief and Suspender Belt Pack. Purple/Black or Red/Black. NYLON 100%.

Purple/Black 10C 220   Red/Black 10H 221
Order sizes: S   M   L
to fit waist: 23/24 25/26 27/28 ins.
Brief/Suspender Belt Pack £5·50

7 'Moonlighter' Basque in satin
   and Lycra with hook and eye back
   fastening and adjustable front lacing.
   Detachable shoulder straps and
   suspenders. Gold. NYLON 84%,
   ELASTANE 10%, POLYESTER 6%.
   Order bust sizes: 34A 36A 34B 36B
                      38B 34C 36C 38C
   10R 247
   Basque/Brief Set £14·99

8 'Aristoc' Beauty Spot Stockings to
   fit foot sizes 8½-11 ins. Pack of
   three. Not sold separately. Black.
   NYLON 100%.
   Order size: M
   21W 526   Stockings £3·75

9 Short length lace trimmed
   Camisole Top Nightdress. Approx.
   length 36 ins. Black. NYLON 100%.
   Order sizes: SW W WX
   20G 332   Nightdress £5·99

10 Blouse top and brief Baby Doll
    Pyjamas in a striped fabric.
    Black. NYLON 100%.
    Order sizes: SW W WX
    20B 376   Pyjamas £7·99

Julie Anne

Aristoc
PACK OF THREE

67

little keith lemon

Anyway, a few weeks after the catalogue arrived in the post, some presents that me mam had ordered from the catalogue used to come through t'post and Greg and I made sure we were always there to greet the postman. I can remember a Scalextric coming one year and going, 'Is this for me?' And me mam said, 'no, it's for next-door neighbour, in't it. I'm saving it for 'em.' I remember finding the same box of Scalextric in a kitchen cupboard a couple of weeks later, next to the mop and bucket. So when me mam were out, we'd go downstairs, get the Scalextric out, me and Belly, and we'd play with it whilst keeping one eye on the clock. About ten minutes before the time she'd be home from work I'd say 'right, better put it back now. Did that piece go there or over there?' In the end we decided that she ain't gonna remember what piece goes where, as long as it's shut and the sellotape is back on it, then we'd put it back in t'cupboard. I remember that Scalextric so well. Even our Greg liked it. It were the only boys' toy he actually liked.

I can remember that build up to Christmas as clear as yesterday. As soon as mam went out: 'Right, let's hunt,' and we'd hunt like it were a mission our life depended on. Hunting. Belly would come round and join in. It was like a proper event, almost like Halloween, it should be in the calendar. Me mam never hid them in all different places, just all of them in one place and when we found them we almost felt scared to open them and we'd just end up shouting 'I've found 'em! Found 'em!'

little keith lemon

Then on Monday, when you go to school, you'd ask yer mates:

'D'you know what you've got for Christmas?'

'No.'

'Eh? Ain't you been looking in t'house?'

'No.'

'Well look what I've got – Wurzel Gummidge with changeable heads.'

The best present I ever got were an Energized Batman. I can remember coming downstairs on me birthday and it was placed on the fire. We had a fire that had fake logs on it, and it were just placed on the mantelpiece above it. What a place to put it! It were practically melting! Anyway, me posh mate had an Energized Batman, so I didn't fink I would ever get one so when I did I were overjoyed. It's a Batman figure with a grappling hook. You just pressed a button, the

hook came out and you could hook it onto somet and Batman would actually climb up. That's it really, but it were exciting back then.

There was an Energized Spiderman too and I own that now, I bought it from a car boot once. I remember the same year I got the Energised Batman, Greg got a John Travolta annual and a *Girl's World* one 'cos he liked doing make-up. He liked to brush me hair and try to plait it. But I didn't want plaits, cos they'd give you a headache.

I remember one year, Greg and I got knock-off Action Men from me auntie where all the parts were just a bit off. I can remember finking 'I can't wait till she's gone so we can have a laugh about his weird hands. He cun't hold hand grenades but he could stroke his Chihuahua, like Ken. It were basically a Ken doll in an army suit. Our Greg wasn't bothered if he could hold a hand grenade, no. It was only if it could hold another man's willy, but it couldn't even do that. It could tap another man's willy cos his hands were stuck together like that. Fake Action Man cun't do anything. All he could do was give high fives. Well he couldn't really even do that because his arms didn't move that way. He could do his hair. Real Action Man weren't bothered about his hair, he shaved it all short like Dermot O'Leary. Action Man has Dermot O'Leary hair, I fink. Or Dermot O'Leary has Action Man's hair.

DOES YOURS DO THIS IF YOU "SQUEEZE" IT?

Everything were confusing back then. We had hormones raging around our bodies and we were still discovering our bodies so there was a lot to discuss:

'I've got one of these, have you?'

'Does yours do this if you squeeze it?'

'Have you ever tried this? It feels ace.'

'What does it taste like?'

All the usual stuff.

I remember when we were nine and we had the conversation about foreskins. I had just discovered that some of me mates had a fleshy sock over t'end of their willy. I went to school and we all start exploring our bodies and going, 'Let's have a look at your willy'. 'Eh? Mine ain't got like a sock on t'end of it.' A fleshy sock. I was surprised how many of my friends had foreskins – but at the time I din't even know that they were foreskins. One of me earliest memories is a horrific one. I can remember being circumcised – but I din't really know what that meant at the time. I remember being in a sink full of red water and seeing meself in the mirror and finking, 'I'm just a baby, what's just happened to me? Why is it really hot between my legs?' And I can remember panicking a little bit when I looked down at me prized possession. I was anatomically gifted from a young age and I din't like anyone messing with me bits. Why would I?! These were me crown jewels and even back then I knew they were gonna be dead important to me.

I was in hospicle and it were awful. There were little kids screaming everywhere. After the episode in the sink, I remember being on t'sofa, wrapped up in a blanket and me mam trying to 'coo coo' in me ear to make me feel better. It felt like I had been abused! More importantly, a few years later, when I saw *Roseanne* on telly, they had that same blanket on t'back of their sofa. Roseanne had me blanket! So I was wrapped up in a blanket, which became my blanky, and Roseanne had the same one on her sofa. It were the only good memory of that story. I didn't carry the blanky around like a hormonesexual, I din't do that. Greg did, but not me. I just had it to keep me warm. I recognised that blanket again when I saw the film *ET* and thought, 'now he's wrapped up in me

little keith lemon

blanket'. Me, ET and Roseanne. Who'd have thought we'd all have the same taste?

I remember when Greg had to have his foreskin off like I did and it were good to be able to talk about it man to man, to sort of say, 'yeah, it hurts dunnit, when they cut your skin off.' I fink he looked up to me in that way. I mean, we did use to fall out all the time, but I used to protect him and teach him about the important stuff in life. I were there for him when people shouted rude stuff about him being a hormone and stuff like that. I remember when he first got a tape recorder and he taped *Fame* off television and played it over and over again. It would just be the sound, all crackly. I pulled all the tape out of the tape. 'I'm sick of hearing about paying for things in sweat, Greg.' And we started fighting. But it were a bit like hitting me sister because he couldn't actually fight. I punched him and I felt bad. We are right close now. He loves coming down to visit me in London as he can be as gay as he likes. It is a bit more open down here I fink. He loves it. But when we went out I felt a bit uncomfortable because more guys wanted to get off with me than with him – I felt bad for him.

Anywhere, when I saw Belly's willy had a fleshy sock on t'end, I were a bit panic stricken, like uh-oh, I ain't got one of them. Because I didn't link sitting in the sink full of blood with having no foreskin, I didn't put the two things together. I can remember finking, 'does your cock grow a foreskin? Will I grow one? Why haven't I grown one yet?' I din't know if you *grew* one. It looked right weird. And that's when I asked me other mates who else had one. 'Oh, I ain't.' 'He has.' Belly I already knew had a foreskin, obviously, but Pisshole had one too. Dave didn't have a foreskin though. There were one lad who weren't sure if he had a foreskin or not and he still doesn't know. He kind of had half a foreskin. I don't know why me and Dave din't have foreskins and, to this day, I don't know the pacific reason why our Greg din't have one either. Me mam can't have just had it cut off cos it were the done thing at that time – like a fashion statement! I mean, I always tried to follow trends but this felt like a step too far. I did play with me knob a lot so perhaps that were the main reason. I have always been a sensual and curious person. I used to like to get naked a lot when I were a kid and me mam tells me that I used to run around in t'street naked whenever I got the chance. I guess I've always been proud of me body. Back in t'day, when it was a lot safer and I were just a toddler, she used to just let me run about the close naked!

Little Keith Lemon

Date: No.

I learnt the word <u>smegma</u> today. Smeg. Smeggy willy. Dave said it and I din't know what he were talking about at first and he asked me whether I ever got a cheesy bell. Where the hell does this cheese come from? Where's it come <u>from</u>? Is that another thing I should have and I ain't got?

Date: No.

I've found out what smeg is.
It's a {fridge}. I don't
understand. Better find
out before I get found
out. I don't think I want
it though.

little keith lemon

ISN'T SMEG A FRIDGE?

When you're a little boy all these words – smeg, smegma – they just don't make sense. I din't properly know what smeg is and you daren't ask anyone at that age. Now I'm a bit older I can rightly say that I've never experienced having smeg and that is down to not having the fleshy sock I now know to be foreskin. Thank God for me mam. Obviously, as an adult who has had sex with lots of ladies, I'm glad that I've never had a foreskin. I always fink women prefer no foreskin because if you're with your boyfriend and it's that special time and you're finking, 'he's been good to me lately, I'm gonna give him a blozzer . . .' with a foreskin-less penis you're not gonna experience smegma.

Do you think Ms Mumphnes
would be fit if she let her
hair down, took her glasses off
and shaved her hairy mole?

yeah she's got ace tits.

I know she reminds me of
Samantha Fox but fatter –
Look at cankles on it. She's
got feet like pigs trotters.
Something about her though.

yeah, I would.

You have to test things out when you're a kid, don't you? You need to find out if you're the only one, compare notes but without revealing that you don't know somet that everyone else knows. It is an art. I remember having the same chat with Dave and Frank the first time I had a double jetty, you know, the first time you don't have a single stream. I was pissing both ways. I din't know if that was just in me mind or I had made it up so I had to ask them if they had ever had it. Now, I'm older and wiser I know the science behind this phenomenon. For anyone who is a man reading this that does have a penis – that would make them a man – they'll know what I mean about a double jetty. If you don't know what I mean let me tell you what I mean: Let's imagine you've been pumping fist to *Babe Station* before you went to sleep. You wake up the next morning, you go t'toilet for a wee and you'll have a double jetty. The science behind this is that the jizm will have blocked up your hole creating a double jetty. To overcome this you have to push a bit harder until it goes to a singular stream. That's a double jetty.

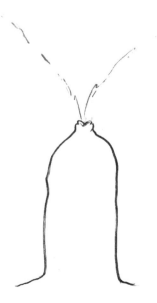

Any man who is reading this knows what I'm talking about. Girls, you're learning. The same fing happens if you've had sex as well. If you have sex and then go for a wee straight after, you won't have a double jetty because your jizm hasn't had a chance to set yet. It is like the jizm kind of glues your end up. If you have a wank into a tissue and then you clean your hole, you just wank into a tissue and throw t'tissue in t'toilet. But what many females don't know is that a lot of times, I'll say about 10 minutes after, you might get a little extra spit. There's a bit more for you. Same as when you have a wee. Dave were always panicking about having a crop circle, especially in the days when we all wore chinos. His knob always gave a bit of an extra spit at the end. I'm sure he won't mind me telling yer. He'd put it away, finking he'd finished and after a bit a little circular wet patch would appear on his chinos ... I can remember him having a wee in a working men's club when we were sixteen, it was some Christmas do, and he were shaking it right thoroughly at t'end to make sure it din't dribble and an old man at the side of him said, 'Hey lad, don't shake it too much, you'll end up doing summat else!' What else did he fink he were gonna do with it? We took the piss out of him for months. 'Dave were having a wank in the loos! In the working men's club!' But we all learned a lesson: you can't shake your knob for too long after doing a piss otherwise it looks like you're having a wank, dunnit?

83

LESSONS YOU DON'T LEARN AT SCHOOL

I don't fink anyone knows the correct way of shaking your willy. Sometimes you shake it fully holding it and sometimes you just hold it a bit – like hold a bit of skin and shake it. No one teaches you that at school, do they? I fink they should make that part of a class at school. When I were younger, I should have just dabbed it with some tissue. I do that now sometimes – but no one is there to tell you these tricks, are they? It's a question I've often asked me mates – 'do you wipe your knob when you have a wee, know what I mean?' I tell you, you'd be surprised how many lads do but they don't suggest doing that when you're a kid.

But the first time I actually had a date with Madame Palm were after playing basketball in me garden and Frank said, 'have you ever pulled your dick loads of times and white stuff comes out and it feels ace?' I said, 'no. I'm just off t'toilet for a wee.' And then I didn't have a wee. I pulled me knob loads of times and white stuff came out and it felt ace and I went, 'yeah, it's ace innit!' Feels like you're gonna piss yourself but it's sexy. And then wanking was introduced. I had a new hobby! I can remember talking about it with Dave and he said he got so excited sometimes that he shoves his thumb up his arse. But to this day I've never shoved me thumb up me arse. When I had piles, after riding a camel, I went t'doctor, that's the first time a finger has been

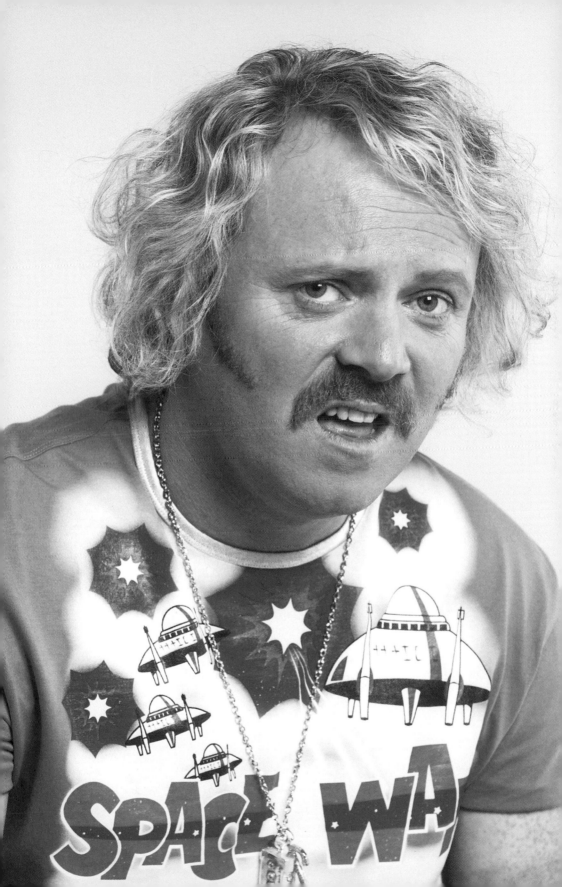

in my anus. When that doctor put their finger in
my anus it felt like it was in me chest. I'm not joking.
I remember she said, 'relax a little bit so I can get in'.
And I said, 'this is as relaxed as it gets. I'm gonna
probably snap your finger off. I can't relax. It hurts and
it feels wrong.' And at that point, I thought Dave would
have loved having piles then. He loved a bit of thumb
up his arse. Every time we'd call for him and knock on
his door after that we said 'Right, Dave, you put your
thumb up your arse? You coming out?' Poor bastard
probably wished he'd never said anything.

By the end of St Michael's we were beginning to
understand what all our different bits did but we
were now ready to learn how to use them properly.
The bad news was that we were heading for an all
boys high school. What was that about?! Me mam
could already see that I were a bit of a hit with
the ladies so she probably thought that it were
a good idea to limit it a bit. It felt cruel at the time.

ALL BOYS SCHOOL

But even though there weren't any lasses at school, when we were eleven we were about to have some of the most fun years of our lives.

Belly and I both lived so close to our high school, Harlington High, so we could both go back to his house at lunchtime. He could literally just climb over the fence at the bottom of his garden and we'd be in. He used to like going home for lunch because he were a fussy eater. Strange for a big lad! But he used to hide the food he din't like down his pants! He were like Napolean Dynamite with Tater Tots in his pocket. What are Tater Tots anyway? Are they like potato croquettes? The only day he wouldn't miss school dinners was Friday. On Fridays, we had fish and chips. Fish and chips Friday, otherwise known as Food Fight Friday. It were a matter of how many chips you could throw, hit the bullseye – someone else right between the eyes – before the teacher turned round. We used to take it really seriously. I was always pretty good at it and finking back now I guess it were quite good training for Keith vs. Jedward.

I can't imagine what those two were like at school! I remember the first time I met Jedward. It were the weirdest day of me life. They just kept saying 'let's go to Tesco's, there's a Tesco's near here. Let's go to Tesco's, it would be so cool to go to Tesco's.' EH?

I asked them why it would be cool and they looked
at each other and at the same time said 'I don't know
but it would be really cool to go to Tesco's'. Weird.

Afterwards, I remember turning round to the Juice
crew and saying 'were that weird or were it just me?'
and I fink that I had a sixth sense as everyone seem
to fink it were weird too. But now I understand those
dingbats and I love 'em. I love 'em like they are me
brothers. I remember a couple of Christmases ago,
they called me five times on Christmas Day at about
5 o' clock in the morning. 'Hey Keith, Father Christmas
is up! It's Christmas. There's a whole world out there!
Let's go, Keith, let's do this.' Imagine you don't give a
shite what anyone finks of you because your brother,
who is just like you, loves you so much. I'd bum him
I would, but is it a bad thing to bum yourself? I would
anyway, just to see what I'm like. I fink I am a bit of
a mentor to them now. They don't really drink or owt
so I like to take them down t'Rhino and get them a lap
dance. Who else is gonna teach them if it ain't their
uncle Keith?

Anywhere, where were I? Oh yeah, me school dinners.
I used to quite enjoy school dinners and not just
because I were ace at food fights. I pacifically remember
discovering coleslaw for the first time at school, not
knowing it was called coleslaw but loving it. I'd have
lashings of the stuff. I'd have a whole plate of it. You
get shit coleslaw and then you get that nice stuff in a
tub that's a bit more special. Well the school stuff was
more like the special stuff out t'tub. I'd go up for fourths.

But I weren't too fussy. We'd all just bolt up for anyfing
that were left over. When you got back to yer table, it
were like you'd won. Like you'd been hunting and come

back with a wild boar instead of some chocolate cake with some pink sauce. Pink sauce! I'd never seen that before and I've never seen it out of school. You'd get chocolate sponge and they had all different coloured custard: pink custard and green custard. But while everyone else were going back for t'chocolate, I were going back for coleslaw. I've never really had a sweet tooth, I've always liked Scotch eggs and crabsticks.

Apart from bread and butter pudding. I used to love that and remember I had it every day for three years. But I won't eat raisins now. I fink they're disgusting. I fink I must have overdosed on them at school. But I go through stages where I'll eat the same thing over and over. I'll eat it all the time until I hate it. I hate parsnips at the moment. When I go round to me mam's she'll want to make a Sunday dinner on a pancake and she'll still try and sneak a parsnip in there. I'll go, 'Mam, I know they're not chips. You try and palm them off as chips, but chips would never go with Sunday roast anyway, or a fucking pancake for that matter.' Me mam used to serve everything on a pancake – like an extra plate. Very modern.

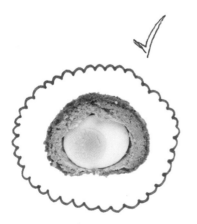

I'VE CAUGHT LONDON

I should say that whilst I am writing this book, I'm eating edamame. As a teenager I would never have known what an edamame was and probably would never have touched it. But I've caught London now and I'm eating edamame and sushi.

When I was growing up my favourite meal was shepherd's pie. We used to have it every Thursday. Thursdays, to me, were best day of t'week because it were shepherd's pie night but also *Kids From Fame* was on and I fancied Coco, who's bi-racial like me. But the black gene touched her more than it touched me. It were the best night of TV all week: *Grange Hill, Top of t'Pops* and *Kids from Fame*. I never really liked *Blue Peter*, I liked the people on the show, and I always remember Yvette Fielding doing the little item about *ET*. No, actually it was Sarah Greene.

I loved *ET*. It was the first film I ever cried at was *ET*. But I don't know how sad it actually was. I fink I worked meself up to being sad just because everyone said it's sad and you'll cry. So at that age, I thought I should cry. I remember I used to go to a cinema and it were 75p back then! 75p! I saw *Sinbad the Sailor* with me mam and our kid. A woman's foot turned into a pig's foot or a duck's foot and I shat my pants to bits so we walked out

little keith lemon

of t'cinema and were confronted with this huge poster for *Jaws*. I can remember testing meself to see how close I could get to it without being scared. But I used to dream that he would crash through the bathroom wall while I were in the bath. I remember telling that to Paddy McGuiness once and he had a similar dream. Mad, in't it?! I also used to fink Freddy Krueger's hand was gonna come up between me legs like in the film. I saw a pirate copy of *Nightmare on Elm Street* and I watched it through so as not to be so scared. You've got to face your fears, haven't you?

I used to tape *Diff'rent Strokes* off the telly with a tape recorder. I didn't have video then so I would just tape the sound and listen to it. I couldn't believe I could tape the sound. Wow! So when videos came out I couldn't believe it at all. How come I can watch any film I want whenever I want? It's bizarre. It used to freak me out. I remember the first video we got. It were *Breakdance*. It inspired me.

ME WAY INTO GIRLS' HEARTS

As there weren't any talent at our school – other than a few fit teachers – we had to find other ways to meet girls, so most of the boys in school used to go to the Youth Club after school on a Friday. It were ace. They used to have disco nights and all the older girls would come along. I always had an eye for the older woman.

By the time we were eleven, I had started to breakdance. I started trying out a few of the spins and stuff at home after watching *Breakdance* the film and then when I found out that the Youth Club were having a talent competition, I thought I'd enter. It din't take long before the girls started to take notice. They were lapping it up! And so I learnt an important life lesson: all men should have a top five list of main primary skills. This is somet you should have prepared when a girl asks you 'what are your top five main primary skills?' Mine are:

1. Having it off
2. Dancing

3. drawing on t'ipad
4. doing the sound of a victorian
bicycle horn
5. skateboarding

Our Greg were a good dancer too. He has still got
aspirations of being a dancer, although I'm not sure
if it will ever happen now. Maybe he needs to go on
Britain's Got Talent or summat. All of the Lemons have
got the moves! Yes, even you Mam. Gregory's a bit tall
though, so when he goes for auditions, I fink he stands
out but not for the right reasons.

TRYST WITH A TEACHER

Before too long I started looking to the older lasses
– those with a bit more experience. One of me teachers,
Miss Birdmuff (she weren't actually called Birdmuff,
but it sounded like Birdmuff to me), I got it on with her.
I knew she wanted to get on with me – it were obvious.
She was like a friendly witch. She dressed like no one
I'd seen before. She had right exotic clothes and she
always wore the same long purple boots. Sexpot.
She'd wear a patterned short skirt, bright coloured
polonecks and neckscarves. She had black, greying
hair and a lot of thick eye make-up on. She looked a bit
like a lesbican version of Claudia Winkleman. Imagine
a lesbican Claudia Winkleman going to a Halloween
party – that's what she looked like.

But her personality was not of a lesbican witch.
She always seemed to like me. She had nicknames
for everyone and I was called Jelly Baby. I don't really
know why. I hope it weren't anything to do with me
looking like an orange jellybaby or a reference to the
colour of me hair, cos as I say it's strawberry blond
not strawberry or ginger. I remember she used to call
Frank 'Old Man'. She used to say things like 'Come
here Little Old Man.' I fink it was because he had the
face of an old man on the body of a young boy.
And she used to call Dave Lettuce. I don't know why.

keith
4
~~dawn~~
miss
birdmuff

Anyway, she taught me how to kiss properly.
I remember when I was younger how wide I used
to open me mouth when I was snogging. I din't know
how wide to open me mouth as I was just graduating
from the pecking style of kissing to full-on snogging.
You don't know, do you? No one really tells you how
wide to open your mouth when you're snogging. I can
remember snogging some girl and we both had our
mouths wide open, so wide I fink her lips might have
been over the top of mine and I felt compelled just to
blow in her mouth. Imagine if I'd have done that, like
mouth to mouth resuscitation. Anyway, Miss Birdmuff
taught me the art of proper kissing and she even
taught me how to pass me chewing gum to her with
my tongue mid-kiss. She was a right classy bird and
that's a trick I still use to this day. The ladies love it.

She was me PE teacher so I used to get a bit of extra-curricular attention in the changing rooms. I didn't enjoy playing sports at school so I had to keep fit through out-of-hours methods – me breakdancing and playing specialist industrial hide and seek with me cousin Gary and some of me other mates that lived in the close. We'd play games that would last for weeks. It were like professional hide and seek. We were too old to be playing normal hide and seek but we thought if we played it industrial-style, it's alright. I often went up trees cos no one would go up to find you if you were in a big tree.

Anywhere, even though Miss Birdmuff had shown me how to appreciate a woman, it weren't quite the same when you were snogging someone your own age. There was a girl who I were seeing for a bit at school, I can't even remember her name so let's just call her Sweet Cheeks, and it were at that time when everyone else was doing the change over from mouth pecking to proper kissing. (It's a good tip that: have a pet name for someone if you can't remember what their name is. My favourite pet name now is butter tits. It is easier to remember one name than a string of different names.) Anywhere, as I said, I was advanced because I'd been there and Miss Birdmuff had shown me how it were done. I knew what to do but if I imposed that on another infant I fink they would have got scared and thought, 'he's too advanced for me'. I always had to be careful not to put girls off with my maturity. So I pulled it back and pretended to act like I din't know what I were doing either. I've always had an older head on me shoulders. I can remember finking, 'I've got to do it now. I've just got to do it now' – but before you stick your tongue in for the first time you can't imagine what you have to do with it, can you? It doesn't make sense

looks like Miss Birdmuff must've taught me a thing or two about PE after all — I won this race against the horse.

to stick me tongue in now, eh? It was easier with
Birdmuff because she would lead the way but when
the other person is doing the pecking style it is hard
to know how to change the style. I remember Sweet
Cheek's sister would point and start laughing at us.
We were standing really straight, not that close to each
other, just our necks forward kissing and trying to work
out what to do with our tongues. Her sister used to say:

'Can you come, Keith, can you come?'
And I'd say, 'Come where?' And they were all laughing.
They just kept saying it, 'Can you come?'
'If you tell me where you're going I'll tell you if
I can come.'
And they'd go, 'No, but can you come?'

They meant 'cum'.

KEITH   DAVE   FRANK

Watched He-Man Masters of the Universe today. What a load of shite. All t'monsters sounded the same and Orco was a reet tit. Imagine if Skeletor was real though. That'd be funny. Funny how He-Man and Skeletor never actually have a punch up. They could sort it out once and for all! I wonder if He-Man could take him? I wonder who would win in a fight between Andi Peters and Jamie Theakston? I bet Andi Peters is surprisingly hard. Wonder if he has it off with Emma Forbes? I would! And that new lass Katy Hill. Got a lovely colour about her. Like a hotdog.

By the way, felt me mate's sister's tits last night. It were ace! Going round there again tonight. Ace times! I love tits. If I had a pair I'd just stay at home all day playing with 'em.

A NEW LANGUAGE

I din't know what they were talking about at the time. But it din't take me too long to find out. It were the same with blow jobs. When you first hear about blow jobs you fink that someone blows your willy, don't you? Still to this day I fink it's the wrong name. It's not a blow job. It's a suck off. The hardest thing about a blow job is trying to understand how to get one. How do you get a blow job? Do you ask for one? Do you push her head down? What do you do? I don't have to ask for them any more, they just happen, but back then you had to ask for it and it came down to persistence. 'Can I have a blow job?' 'No.' 'Why?' It would go round and round until I got one. But then, I remember the first time I actually got one, there were teeth scrapage. Obviously, she din't know what she was doing and I din't know what it was supposed to be like so I can just remember finking, 'that's it. Done it. Now I can tell me mates'. What else are they gonna do with their teeth? They're in there aren't they? They're gonna scrape. I can remember being a bit sore afterwards and she didn't finish it off. She just said, 'that's it'. And I went t'bathroom and had a wank.

Maybe she were scared about having jizm in her mouth or maybe she were scared of the projectile? She might have been scared that it might have made her throw up, like when you put a finger down your throat and it is an instant reaction. It is weird because sometimes it is just a dribble and sometimes it is

little keith lemon

Date: No:

I found another one!
I wasn't sure at first but
it ~~defini~~ definitely is
one! Now I've got
more pubes than Belly.
Can't wait to tell him.

a burst and I don't know what it means. When I were a kid I would often be hitting the headboard. The panic was 'ooo shit, where's it gone? Oh no! Where's it gone!'. I remember coming downstairs once and chatting to my mam for a bit and then looking in the mirror and seeing this dirty mark on me face. It looked like hubba bubba had burst on your cheek and get stuck on your face.

I fink we all learnt at a similar sort of time what things meant. I felt more mature than a lot of the lads in me class but there were a few that were more mature if you took their pubes into account. It was very important to get pubes. I can remember the first people with pubes. They got mocked for having pubes. 'Ah, hairy willy!' And you'd always fink, 'when am I gonna get a brown willy like a dad willy?' Our teacher, Mr Sheep, he had a brown willy. He was a white man with a brown willy. So we used to fink in our minds, we're gonna get a brown willy when we grow up, like as you grow up, your willy gets a tan. But I never got a brown willy. And still, to this day, I don't know if he always had a brown willy or his willy went brown. Or perhaps he's just been having a lot of anal sex. We'd always compare our knobs, like when you'd go to your mate's house. 'Hey, look, I've got about nine pubes now.'

AND HER CHERRY- SMELLING HOUSE

Angela Chase were me first serious girlfriend, when I was twelve. Obviously the girls before that had meant somet to me but I weren't emotionally developed enough to really take it to the next level. I remember her birthday party and her house smelled of cherries, which got stuck in me head – a cherry-smelling house. She was quite posh, well, posher than me anywhere. She probably wanted a bit of rough. But I've never let little things like that stand in my way. I knew she were posh as she had one of those gaint Head bags. It were what all the posh kids had. I didn't have a Head bag. I've often thought, is that around the same time holdalls were invented? Cos it were basically a holdall that kids would use for school. Interesting that, in't it? Those bags were absolutely massive. I could have slept a night in it. Big school bags was a thing, a fashion. But by that age, I had already discovered me own unique style.

Anywhere, the fact that she had one of those giant
Head bags and I didn't have one weren't gonna stand
in my way. I could talk the hind legs of a horse and
managed to win her over with me charm. She was in
the same class as me at school and I knew she were
making eyes at me across the maths classroom.
After class, I just went straight up to her and kissed
her. We kissed for five and a 'alf minutes! I nearly died.
I used her as a snorkel. I could tell she were bedazzled
by me. I fink she were the first person I said 'I would

destroy you' to. She looked a bit like Sandy from *Grease* before she became rock chick Sandy. I liked the girl-next-door Sandy better than rock chick one, me. I've met Olivia Newton-John now, it's mad! She were really nice and gentle with a lovely soft voice, just like she were in me dreams. Anywhere, I told Angela that at the weekends me mam used to take me to a dog rescue place and I could see her eyes melt. Girls love animals, especially brocken ones. She pacifically liked dogs. And horses, even though they are horrible and too big for humans to ride. I know I've talked about Owen Wilson before and people say I look like him but that in't the only thing we have in common. He also used a love of dogs to his advantage. In *Marley & Me*, he shows his softer side by pretending he likes Guide Dogs. And he scored Jennifer Aniston because of it! You can't say fairer than that.

I right liked Angela. Me mam gave me a locket necklace and I gave it to her and I put two pictures of me in. I fink the idea was that you are supposed to have one picture of her and one of me but I knew she'd appreciate having two of me. And I didn't have a picture of her. We didn't have a camera to take a photo of her but I used to draw pictures of her instead. I though it were nice to draw a picture of your girlfriend. It were like, 'I like you, so I've drawn a picture of you.' It's like saying, 'do you want to wear me coat?' innit? When a girl wears your coat and you're a kid you fink, 'I'm in there. She's got me coat on. She's picked me coat up from goalpost. Yeah, I'm gonna kiss her for two minutes.' Anyway, a couple of weeks after giving her the locket, she came round to me house and dropped it off telling me we weren't boyfriend and girlfriend any more. It were like a bolt from the blue. I couldn't believe it. At least she'd brought the

locket back but I'd missed Frank's birthday so I could draw that picture of her. I was heartbroken and then I bought a plasticine Hulk kit and got over it. Some of me mates have told me that it's horrible when you get dumped. Your heart feels like it is broken into a million pieces – your pride shat on all over the floor. But I fink you've just got to pick yourself up and get over it. Don't fink too much about it. You can play it to your advantage if you are a bit clever about. Some girls like it if you are broken, they like to be able to help fix you. If you are lucky, she will want to try and help fix you physically. You'll soon forget about your problems. Anywhere, the best advice I can give to anyone who finds themselves being dumped is to go on t'rebound. Some people spend their whole life on the rebound and they are getting a lot of action. And if you're not looking for anything too serious, it can mean you can punch above your weight, getting some tidy totty that would normally be out of your league. And sometimes it can develop into somet bigger, if you play your cards right. I often fink that when I see famous couples. Jay-Z and Beyonce are a prime example. Surely Beyonce was on the rebound when she first got with Jay-Z? She is stupid fit. I'd let her kick the crap out of me.

This isn't the plasticine
Hulk I got, this is another
one me mam got me.
I had two Hulks.

PLAYING TO ME STRENGTHS

I wasn't a star pupil educationally. I was always playing the joker and I talked a lot but I weren't naughty just cheeky. I would question a lot of things – always asking why:

Teacher: We're doing algebra.
Me: Why? What job will I need algebra for?
Me: When does a letter become a number?
Me: What? I'm not gonna need this in my job, I know I'm not.
Teacher: Comment t'apelle tu?
Me: Eh? I don't need French, sir.
Teacher: You might go to France …
Me: Well, if I do I'll ask someone there.
Teacher: Religious Education.
Me: Why?

But even if I weren't a straight-A student, I have always had many other skills. I have always thought the main purpose of going to school was to learn some social etiquette. I don't fink I would be the man I am today if it hadn't been for the lessons I learnt at school. For instance, I used to sit skinny Peter Wright, a boy from my class, on me knee and pretend he was a puppet that would talk back to me … Kind of like a ventriloquist fing. Everyone were laughing and we didn't prepare a fing. We just did it. He moved around and I threw him around a lot and asked him questions. We did the water trick and I'd say, 'do you wanna try some talking now and I'll give you some water?' That's what they do, ventriloquists, don't they? So he were spitting water out at everyone and I can remember finking, 'Wow, all you need to do is spit at the audience and they'll laugh at it, it's easy this in't it?!' I've used that trick a few times – once with some Weetabix. I won a competition at me mate's house, who could eat the most dry Weetabix – I started laughing and it sprayed everywhere. I fink that gave me my first taste of what it would be like to be an entertainer.

I had an ace time at school today. Mick got a detention because he threw a brick at Mr. Price! It weren't on purpose. All the dingbats from the bottom set were throwing bricks over school but it were just a shame for him that he hit Price! He said it were funny though. He said he made a noise like a seagull being hit with a brick. 'Aaah.'

At high school everyone got on. When you hear about bullying these days I find it hard to understand because we had no bullying. All the dickheads were dickheads and we loved 'em for being dickheads. It weren't like we were all the same either. There was a hierarchy, for instance, the posh kids shopped at Next because Next was a different world.

Anyone with a Next jumper, I just remember finking 'bloody hell, they're posh aren't they?' but you didn't have a go at them for it, and they don't care that you don't shop in Next.

Come to think of it,
Mick were like the
original Joey Essex.

It were the teachers that you had to look out for. If you were caught chatting in class or whatever, the teacher would turn round and throw chalk at you. I fink you could have physical contact when I was at school and they'd hit you. Pummel you, or flick your ear. I remember one teacher in particular, Mr Standish, used to pull your ear and flick it. And he was bald but he'd combed his hair from the back forward and when we went swimming his hair flowed behind him like a mermaid. 'He's got no hair . . . Standish's got no hair! Standish's a baldie!' But his hair went down his back because he'd grown it at the back, grown it there and combed it right up. I've heard of a comb-over but a comb-back?!

The only piece of advice I would give kids at school is if they are getting bullied, don't take it too seriously unless it turns into violence. If you have the balls, just say, 'fuck you' straight away and then they'll go, 'Oh, we can't bully him because it stops there.' If you have the balls, just say it. Straight away. Say 'fuck you and fuck off! Go fuck yourself you fucking fuckster'.

PERFECTING ME PLAYGROUND FLIRT

There were other lasses after that but I weren't really keen to tie meself down to one girl in particular. I don't fink anyone should when they are young. You're only young once! I was always just looking for a bit of fun.

I used to enjoy flirting with girls whether I got together with them or not. Often if I fancied someone, I would punch them in the face and set their hair on fire. 'Eh, your hair's on fire. I fancy you.' The method of flirtation was basically take the piss out of them and before you knew it, you've scored. You should try it! At school, one of the girls in my class Natalie, wrote me a letter asking me out and I wrote back and said, 'eff off, you dog' and showed me mates and sent it back. Then afterwards I thought, 'oh no, I fancy her loads, why was I such a dingbat?' so I said to her 'I just don't know how to be around girls, I don't want the other boys to see how much I like you cos I'm very sensitive.'

It din't work every time but it usually got their attention. This way of flirting I still use to this day. Take for instance on *Celebrity Juice* when I give Fearne a lot of grief about her massive nostrils. I do this as I properly fancy her so I try to belittle her so I can control my emotions towards her. She's an inspiration that woman. She does a lot of work for charity. I fink a lot of girls aspire to be her but with smaller nostrils. I have a lot of respect for that woman. I don't want to marry her or anyfing, but I do want

Little Keith Lemon

to have a go on her. I bet she's a right one in the bedroom. I've always said it: nice girl-next-door image but in the sack a proper dirtbag. I use the same technique on Stacey Solomon. I call her a sexy rodent – it sounds like abuse but I am actually paying her a compliment. Try it!

When I were doing the research for this book, I came across a shoebox full of the letters and poems I used to write to girls to win 'em over. I wrote this one to Melanie, a girl who were in me class.

Sexy Rodent

Dear Melanie,
You sit only two seats away from me
at school and I know sometimes I am
silly in class and get me knob out but
you are the prettiest girl I have ever
seen. Even prettier than Wonder Woman.
The next time I get my knob out, I would
be really grateful if you let me put it
in your shoulder. I don't really know
what love is but I have strong feelings for
you that I think are love. Its not pervy,
me putting me knob on your shoulder,
Its love. I think I love you Melanie.
                        Keith x

Dear Keith,
You are a fucking dickhead. The next time
you get your knob out in class I am going
to smack it with a shatterproof ruler.
I have already told Mrs. Thompson about
you getting your knob out, you should
have a letter home to your parents.
Don't _ever_ speak to me again.
                              Melanie

Dear Melanie
I am so upset that me getting me knob
out has offended you in any way. It is
very immature of me but at this
difficult time in our lives where we are
getting spotty skin and hairs in all sorts
of areas, I feel I can't express meself
unless I get my knob out. I would
really like to take you for McDonalds.
My mate works there and we will get
free chips. Keith x

Even if I fancied you Keith I would never go to McDonalds because I am sure that McDonalds is responsible for half of our rainforests being destroyed. I saw it on John Craven's Newsround. It might just be propoganda but I don't like their clips anyway. I prefer chunky chips

What the fuck is propooganda? Do you want to go out or what?

Yeah ok.

Which obviously meant she fancied me.

So I took her swimming. It is a great way to get to know someone really quickly and see if you can take the relationship any further. Even though we were only fourteen, she had a body like a twenty-nine-year-old. She was Tick, tickety boo. I paid for everything like a gent, gave her a pound for her locker and bought her a hot chocolate and some mini cookies afterwards. She thought I were the don. I poked her and didn't wash me hand for a week. But it smelt more like swimming baths.

Every time I go to swimming baths now, it reminds me of Melanie.

Here are some of the other notes I found in the shoebox. I would tell you who they all are but I can't remember them so you'll just have to imagine what they all looked like. Imagine an even fitterer version of Martine McCutcheon.

Dear Molly

Everyone talks about your tits. I do too,
I love your tits to bits.
I love the shape, I'd like t'see them in
a batman cape.
Nowt else, just that alone. You mek
me stiff I get a bone.
Meet me after school.

Keith.

charlotte Needs, I bet you
have needs.
I bet I can satisfy (your
(needs.)
I am a gifted man oh yes.
I am, my cock is fick
as a coke can.
Hope t'see you at the
youth club this Friday
                    X X

TINA

Lovely Tina I cun't be
keener to flick your
beaner, know what I
meaner?
Wanna meet in the cantina
You have me desert, and
me can of pop, on me list
of fit birds you are top.
You have ACE tits.
                  Keith x

Dear Claire.
You have nice hair.
I wanna kiss your tits and flick your bits
I mean that in the nicest way.
So how about it, what d'ya say.
If ya give me a blow job
I won't tell me mates no matter how
long it takes.
I'd wait for 3 wks or if more,
I'll never fink you're a dirty whore.
You are so fit, how about it, can
I kiss your big juicy tit?
Left or right not bothered.

Keith x

CAN I BUY YOU A GOLD LABEL?

little keith lemon

I wouldn' actually have ever said that. Buy your own own Gold Label – I've only got a few quid. But I like the idea that I were a gentleman, putting the ladies first, even back then. I fink we were about thirteen or fourteen when we started to discover alcopops and super-strength lagers. We realised that if we had a few bottles of that stuff before we went out, in our heads we became the best-looking boys at youth club. The first time I got drunk was in t'park, on alcopops: Mad Dog, Twenty Twenty, Breezers – all of it at once until our teeth dropped out. I can remember going home and walking through t'living room. I had mud on me jeans and on me hands as I'd fallen over a few times on t'way home. I were pretending not to be drunk in front of me mam. 'I'm off to bed, goodnight Mam.' I just walked straight in. No chat. She knew! I remember the next morning I were still puking me guts up on Mad Dog and saying 'I'm never drinking that stuff ever again.' And I din't. I fink me mam were a bit worried that I'd get in trouble if I were drunk, but at least I din't take drugs! That's cos I grew up in the era of Zammo singing *Just Say No*.

We used to go to park all the time and there were a little wooden gazebo type fing. It had seats in and it was all wood so you were under shelter. It would be filled with teenagers all just getting off with each other. Just feeling tits for hours. But it was weird how everyone just shared – the lads and the lasses. Because

it weren't your girlfriend and you'd try not to like 'em too much because you knew you'd go there next week and she'd be sat on someone else's lap and you'd fink, bastard. What am I supposed to do? Just let it go? Then you'd ask another girl to sit on your lap. And before too long you could ask: Do you want to go for a walk?

That wooden gazebo in t'park were also the site of many games of spin the bottle. They were good years, there weren't that much hassle about the whole thing – it weren't like you were girlfriend-boyfriend, were you? You just snogged, and occasionally you might clean the windows. A game not traditionally associated with snogging is Murder-word but it always worked for me. Basically, to play Murder-word, you needed two teams and each team would have a word. Then you had to get a letter out of the person to spell out their word. It were quite advanced and educational at the same time, weren't it? So you might tickle them to death to get their letter out of them or go, 'I wanna snog you'. If you're lucky you might get a girl who says, 'I don't care'. And then you snog. And you go, 'You know what? You can keep your fucking letter. Keep it. I don't want your letter. I wanna feel your bangers.' 'I don't care.' 'Right. Well, here's me letter, it's S.' When we got a bit older, you might get to finger-blast someone.

I fink it were around the same time that I started to fink about dressing to impress the ladies. I used to spend all me pocket money on *Star Wars* figures when I was at St Michael's, I used to have loads of them all lined up. And then I got to high school, started going to Youth Club and drinking alcopops and I thought, I am gonna sell me *Star Wars* figures cos I like clothes now, so I can get some fanny. Because I weren't gonna get any fanny with *Star Wars* figures, were I?

I had a paper round from the newsagent at the bottom of the hill, Bottom Shop as we called it, and that gave me a bit more spending money for clobber as well. We didn't have a corner shop because where I lived there were no corners. So it was just Bottom Shop and Top Shop. And top shop was one of those shops that sells everything. I still love those shops now. It would get right Christmassy over Christmas and you wonder where they'd stashed all the other stuff. I used to love going in. I never knew what I were gonna buy, just knowing there would be summat in there that I'd need. I go to B&Q now for the same reason. I wander round, I'm not after anything, but I'll see somet and go, that'll come in handy. 'Have you got any really strong double-sided sticky tape?' 'Yeah, I have actually. I don't know why I bought it but I knew it'd come in handy for somet.' 'Have you got any spray that'll go onto plastic garden chairs?' 'Yeah.'

But the newsagent in bottom shop was like Frank Carson. He didn't have catchphrases or anything like that but he really looked like him. Obviously, the temptation was to dump your bagful of papers and say someone stole your bag, but I learnt a good lesson about honesty doing that paper round. Rather than dumping the bag and lying about it, I used to set little challenges for meself. I'd time meself so I could do the quickest round possible and then go back to the shop quicker than I had the day before. I fink I am a good law-abiding citizen and it paid off as that kept me in decent clobber for a bit. I now shop in Zara, Top Man, River Island and asos. I like Selfridges a lot cos the sales assistants are fit. I had a go on one in the changing rooms once and she gave me a discount after, so that were nice!

>> LOOKING <<
THE PART

I've said it before and I'll say it again, the rules of
attraction are simple: you have to be attractive.
And if you are not attractive, you've got to dress up
as someone who is. Style is as important as the tiny
arms on a T-rex. Without style you are not stylish. And
if yer not fit, just dress up as someone who is. Easy. My
look was inspired by different style icons fused with
my own sense of fashion. Wearing the right clobber is
a big part of that. It's what's on the outside that decides
if you will get inside, if you know what I mean.

People knew who I were back in those days – and it is
the same these days. Back then, when everyone else
were wearing jeans or chinos, I wore a suit. I wore as
much flamboyancy then as I do now. My favourite
party outfit was a suit with one leg that was red, one
leg that was black and it had red arms. It was a safari
jacket with a belt and everything. I felt dead good in
that outfit and if you feel good, you are confident and
you are good. If I am not 100% happy with what I am
wearing, I don't feel as good. If you feel stylish, you
feel confident, I fink.

Once I found £15 in the street and I must have been
about thirteen so £15 felt like £300 or more. I went into
Leeds and Belly was with me, I gave him a fiver and
I kept the tenner. We went into town to a shop called
Class and I bought some bottle-green jumbo cords,
some deck pumps with a palm tree pattern on and
I bought a green roll neck with a zip. Head to toe in

134

little keith lemon

green. I always knew how to make a statement. It is back then that I learnt that a big part of being a style guru is knowing how to wear clothes, not just what to wear. If you can't carry off an outfit, you'll look like a right nonce. I strutted my way round Leeds market in that green concoction and if you don't know what strutting is let me tell yer what it is. It is walking with a swagger. Pick a song in your head and walk to that beat, stride with rhythm, it looks good.

I often used to pick a Duran Duran song as Simon Le Bon always held himself well. He looks like he has just walked out of River Island. He's got a good barnet, too, which helps. I was blessed with having strawberry blond hair which goes mainly with any colour. My hair was always thick and lustrous so I could carry off most dos. Gingers don't have the same luck – their ginger hair always clashes with everyfing and makes them look like geeks.

I remember going through a stage in me life where you would take labels off of fings and sew them onto other fings, like Le Coq Sportif. At around the same time there was a fad for nicking VW signs off of VW cars. We were inspired by the Beastie Boys. Frank and I used to go out and swipe them. I felt like the devil! But it was encouraged back then by pop culture. You had 'em round your neck as trophies. I collected three of them. A little one, a normal size one and a big fuck off massive one. And everyone was doing it and I'm not saying if everyone took drugs, I'd take 'em but to get yer hands on one of them fings was a pretty big deal. Anywhere, at school, the headmaster found out about it and the police came to talk to us to tell us we were stealing and vandalising people's property, and in our heads it didn't even register. We just thought, 'eh? No,

we're just looking cool like the Beastie Boys. Beastie Boys have done it. They've got proper jobs and they're doing it'. Anyway, they said they were setting up a box where you could bring in your VW signs – like an amnesty. I just buried mine in the back garden instead, I felt too guilty to admit that I'd stolen them in the first place.

It were the same time that bomber jackets were in fashion with badges all over. I fink I was a bit reminiscent of Tom Cruise in *Top Gun*. I used to hang around in Dortmund Square chatting up the birds and cos I came from a one-parent family, I had a cheaper version of a bomber jacket, it din't seem to have enough padding in. This girl I was trying to get off with, Melanie, I fink her name was, had a full, puffy one. There was a scale from t'budget ones right up the banging puffy ones. But again, it din't matter too much as it is more about how you wear it than how puffy your bomber jacket is. And when I teamed the bomber with a pair of PVC crocodile-skin jeans, all shiny, Melanie couldn't keep her hands off me. Sucked me t'hinge end in't toilets.

These days I'm trying to bring back some of the clothes that I got lucky in when I was kid – fings like Boy and Destroyer. And it's not just clothes, I've got a new Raleigh Burner recently. It's gold with all the competition tubing and me mam couldn't afford it when I were a kid, but now they have reissued it and I can relive me youth. It has become me chosen means of transportation. One of me Leeds mates came down and now I've got two BMXs so we went out for a ride just like we did when we were kids. I felt like I had arrived. That's what fame and fortune have bought me. Two BMXs.

I had a bit of a routine before I went out. The main part of that routine were that I sprayed on a lot of Lynx. It were the only thing I knew back then. I did graduate to Paco Rabane aftershave when me auntie bought it for me, but I were only ten . Ten! Aftershave when you are ten! I had a thick line of downy hair but I weren't gonna shave cos I wanted that to grow! I din't understand until I were a bit older that you had to start shaving to make it less fluffy. I din't need aftershave. I suppose I was mature for me age so they got confused.

SHAVING ME HAIRS

I was always that bit more advanced than me mates so I had to start shaving before most of them were even out of nappies. I din't use to make a big fuss about it or owt but other lads did. It were one of those things that people used as a sign of their manhood. 'Ave you started shaving? Ave you fingered a girl yet?'... that sort of thing.

I must have had about four hairs on me chest when I started shaving me face and I remember finking 'I'll shave them off as well. Don't need them, do I?'. And overnight, I sprouted this thick carpet of hair across me chest! I remember people saying that if you shave yer chest, it grows back thicker and it is true. Plus, as a teenager, you want to shave, don't yer? As an adult, you don't want to shave and you don't want any pubes, do you? You know what I mean? You don't want any pubes in summer time when it's hot. Ooof!

But I never used to trim me pubes, not until me mate Jade told me he trimmed his. 'Oh, you bender, you trim yer pubes? And then I can remember one day I was really hot and I just trimmed 'em. I was trimming me tache anyway so I thought I would just trim the rest while I were at it and it made a real difference. But first time you trim your pubes they go a bit spiky and sharp. But they don't now, especially if you use a bit of conditioner to keep them in good condition. It's like a Pantene advert down there!

We did have sex education classes at school where we learnt all about puberty, pubes and pregnancies. Everyone said that Ms Johnson got her tit out in it so we were well excited. Ms Johnson set a law: 'if you laugh or giggle I will ask you to leave the room' so I nearly just got up and walked out there and then saying 'Miss, I'm going to piss meself I can't help it' but then I'd miss Ms Johnson's bangers. I just remember finking, 'When's she gonna get her tit out, man? I thought she gets her tit out?' I can remember Frank got kicked out for giggling. I was finking, 'Please don't giggle, don't giggle. I haven't seen Mrs Johnson's tit.' Imagine ruining it by giggling and being sent out and then, 'did you see Mrs Thompson's tit?' 'No, I got kicked out for giggling.' Bastard!

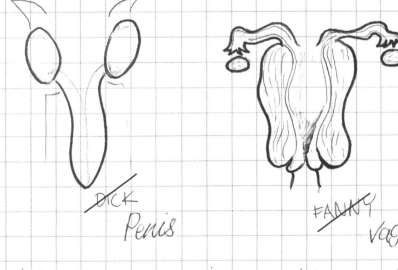

DICK
Penis

FANNY
vagina

Keith, how many times do I have to tell you to use the scientific names?

A lot of people have a popular misconception of me that I am highly sexed. I'm not, I am just very honest. When I was youngerer before I became sexually active, I was embarrassed about it. I felt like if I became sexually active me mam wouldn't love me any more as she'd fink she had lost her little boy. So I remember rushing me sex education homework so I din't have to do it at home in front of me mam. They made us do these scientific drawings of vaginas and penises. The penis looked like an evil fox and my vagina looked like a tryphid. I fink they made you do sex education to scare you off sex. I remember looking at me scientific drawing of vagina and finking, I would never put me dick in that! It would bite it off, it looks like a sarlacc from *Return of the Jedi*.

ME TEACHERS

MR BILLDERCH

Billderch were a small fella and he had a tash. Almost all me teachers had a tash. As he were one of the PE teachers I very rarely saw him in anyfing else but a tracksuit. He wasn't as harsh as some of t'teachers but he did make us take our trunks off in t'showers which was a bit odd. I remember one of me mates who had no pubes drew his on with a pen. I pissed meself when they came off in t'shower.

MR ROXBRIDGE

Another PE teacher, but he also did Maths. I never understood that. Once he caught me cutting through t'park doing cross country. We were supposed t'go around t'park. But in my defence he never said you cun't go through t'middle. I thought I was beating t'system. But all I really was doing was inviting a detention. Which I talked me way out of. Mr Roxbridge was a skinny fella who looked a bit like the weasel from *Wind in t'Willows*, and he stunk of fags. He would sometimes smoke whilst out doing cross country with us. He shouted at me a lot on t'football pitch but I din't care if we won or lost. Football isn't my cuppa tea. Neither is tea.

MISS PANTHORPE

Quite young for a teacher. She were the only female teacher at high school so we obviously thought she was fit. She looked like a rough Belinda Carlisle. She had a hairy mole as well unlike Belinda Carlisle. But, Belinda Carlisle was fit. I wonder how she earns her money now? It was rumoured that Panthorpe got her tit out in science but I never saw it.

MR MONNINGTON

Monnington taught Maths and English. He used to repeat everyfing he said under his breath. Really strange. Would head pummel ya if ya pissed about. He wore tweed head to toe. Bet he even wore tweed underpants. Must've been some reason he was pissed off. Imagine tweed under crackers ... Fuckin 'ell that'd drive yer nuts!

MR LINCH

Foreign bloke who looked like a snake. He would throw chalk at ya if he caught you talking in class. I weren't mad on him. He always wore Slazenger jumpers.

MR LAWRENCE

He did woodwork. Looked like a garbage pail kid.
It were like a baby's head on a man's body. He were
a proper Yorkshire bloke. The good fing about his class
though, were that he'd have t'radio on in class. I liked
that. Right low like but ya could hear it. He dressed
old-fashioned like most of t'teachers. Teachers were
different back then, they proper looked and smelt
like teachers. Coffee breath.

MR DARKWOOD (AKA BATMAN)

The headmaster. Old school. He actually wore a cape!
In a good mood he was ok. Bad mood, I'd rather go
t'prison than be sent t'his office. He looked like an
American eagle. Grey hair. I say hair but it was like
wool. He had a pointy, angry face. On t'wrong side
of him and ya were fucked. Could well have been
a murderer acting as a teacher.

MR GREENHILL

Obviously hadn't bought any new clothes since the
seventies. He were balding but he had long hair at
t'back. Really thick glasses. Could've easily been in
Cheech and Chong. He looked like a stoner and was
very easy going, just let you get on with it. He was
more like a mate than a teacher. Smelt a bit off but
ya just din't stand too close t'him.

POSTER GIRLS

Hey, I've found this photo of me bedroom. Me walls used to be covered with pictures of women. Kylie was up there! It was when she was singing 'I should be so lucky'. My mate said she looks like a goofy fashion bunny. But I was there from the start. When Michael Hutchence got hold of her, he turned her round. I can remember seeing her in some Levi 501s and finking she has got the best arse I have ever seen. You rarely saw that kind of arse in real life, how she wore those jeans back then. I fink it were because they were a bit high-waisted and it really accentuated a lady's curves. It were a bit different cut weren't it? But she always used to wear knackered 501s, and I remember her red leather jacket on t'front of *Smash Hits*. Seeing that photo, I thought, 'yeah, I'm nearly in love with you and I don't even know you so that's weird.' I thought I were never gonna meet her, but that's why you were allowed to be so obsessed with famous people – because you knew you were never gonna meet them, so you're allowed to like 'em more than a normal person. When you know someone, it's a bit different. I mean, Holly still sometimes looks at me and rips all me clothes off with her eyes. I can see it. She's got desire for me. I can see that but it is different when you see someone day in day out. I used to fink Fearne fancied me but I'm gonna have to work at that one. I fink I've lost that out me grasp now. She's all loved up. I don't want to go out with someone who's had a baby. She must look like a bin liner down there. Or even worse a bucket. Or a pint glass. I know I am as thick as a Coke can ... but a Coke can that will fit in a pint glass and still have room for a couple of pens.

I don't fink of them sexually but I feel really flattered that I hang around with such lovely looking ladies and I fink a lot of men are jealous that I do.

Patsy were another one that featured highly on me wall of course. That woman is so fit it cancels itself out. She were in a band called Eighth Wonder at the time. I were proper obsessed with Patsy. I know her now. She's a good mate of mine. If she ever wants to be more than just mates, it's her call.

CHEAP THRILLS

I remember the first time I got a bit excited by Jenny Agutter in the shower in *American Werewolf in London* and me mam asked me to make a cup of tea but I cun't get up. She would have seen I had happy pants. I wrote a letter of complaint t'BBC for showing such a sexually graphic film without warning.

Keith Lemon
36 Brudenell Close
Leeds

Hello Sir
I would like to make a complaint about the American Werewolf in London. There is no warning of the sexual content but when Jenny Agutter was in the shower it were extremely arousing. When me mam asked me to make her a cup of tea, I was unable unable to do so. I could have burnt me penis and blinded me mam with it all at once. Please put a warning in future.

Keith Lemon

Another film that got me tingling down below were one of the craziest films I've ever seen in me life, *Xanadu*. Olivia Newton-John is in it and she is so super bang in it that it shouldn't be allowed. I met her on Jonathan Ross and I told her. I thought the film was amazing and I still watch it. But I don't like the story. I just really like her. She was lovely. And Belinda Carlisle, obviously. I had a door poster of Belinda Carlisle. A long, thin door poster. I would go to HMV and Athena and spend an hour in there choosing posters. There was the classic tennis player shot, scratching her arse, which I've lampooned many times, or a man holding a baby. But whenever I fancied a famous person, I'd just fink I want to go out with someone who looks like her.

There were a film called *Perfect*, which starred John Travolta and Jamie Lee Curtis and a lot of high-leg leotards. That also used to send me blood rushing to me willy end. I remember at the time, Jamie Lee Curtis was rumoured to have both a tuppence and a tallywhacker. Anyway, I fink it is all the stuff of nonsense otherwise she wouldn't have known what to do when she went to the toilet – stand up, sit down, stand up, sit down. It's just like Lady Gaga. Some people say she is one of those marmafrodites. But she in't. I saw her at the BRITs and she got her bits out.

When I were youngerer, I were much more into film than I were into music but I do remember what the first record I ever bought were. They always ask you that in t'interviews, don't they? Not sure how interesting that is but anywhere. My first record was *Joshua Tree* and maybe I'm not as cool as I thought I was because I went back the next week and bought Terence Trent

D'Arby *According to the Hard Line*. That were
probably me black roots kicking in. I felt a connection.

The first ever gig I went to were at Roundhay Park
to see Michael Jackson. I couldn't afford a ticket,
so I went with my scally mate who used to nick
jeans off washing lines he knew someone who knew
someone who could get us in. He didn't say it was
through a sewage pipe though. And he got in stinking
of shit! I said, 'I ain't going through a sewage pipe
to get in,' so a couple of us climbed up a tree and we
could see in anyway. We were just up a tree watching.
He was inside but he stank.

It were a couple of years later that I went to a gig
and actually had a ticket. There were a big group
of us Leeds lads who went down to London on a
coach to see INXS. It were one of the best days of
me life and there weren't even any birds there! Just
a load of blokes wondering round trying to look
like Michael Hutchence.

If you ever see *Live Baby Live* or *Live Baby Live* ...
Live and live, same thing innit? It's spelt the same
so I never knew what to call it. I'm on it. I got t'front.
We went in and we just ran to the front, squashed
against the barrier. It were only 10am! At about 11.30
I needed a piss and I looked back – and I'd never seen
so many people in me life. I thought there's no way
I'm gonna go back there for a piss. I'll never get
back here so I just sucked it back in. Back then I had
a bumbag on and every time I jumped up, the bumbag
stuck in me pissbag, in me pisswomb and made it
worse. I know what yer finking – you wore a bumbag?
What a dingbat! But it were the fashion to wear
a bumbag back then – or I made it a fashion.

Anyway, I din't go for a piss ALL DAY! It would have been a better day if I'd have just laid down on t'floor and dug a hole and done a piss into that. But I needed a piss all t'way through. I can remember when it had finished we got on the coach to go back to Leeds and I was pissing in a Coke can and I said, 'give me that bin liner' – there were a bin liner for rubbish – 'give me that bin liner because I'm gonna fill it' and then I kind of just put the bin liner onto me penal area and just pissed in the bin bag. And yeah, it were the longest piss I've had in me life. I remember finking I could have got one of those Guinness World Records for the longest piss into a bin bag ever.

THE BAKERY IS NOT THE BEST PICK-UP JOINT - UNLESS YOU FANCY GRANNYS

Our school made us do work experience and we all had to troop off and do two week's work experience in the summer. I never understood it because they sent me to a bakery. Shouldn't it be somet that I actually wanted to do when I grew up? I don't want to be a baker! No offence to any bakers out there, but I weren't going to waste this face on being a baker. I were making sandwiches with women that were old enough to be me Auntie Jean. Am I fucking making sandwiches with me Auntie for a job?!

They were all old women. I thought it might be a good opportunity to pull birds but they were all old women. There were one other girl who were the same age as me who were there to do work experience too but she had a wob eye. If you talked to her for too long her eye would go off t'other way. I couldn't do that, I just din't know where to look at her. I just looked at the floor in embarrassment. She were right nice though, I wonder what she's up to now. I would definitely bang her now. I wouldn't let that eye stand in me way.

All the others were me mam's age. I often thought, 'when will I fancy mams?' And now I'm in me late twenties (ok, I'm in me thirties), I fink I am starting to fancy mams. Unless mams have got fitter. I wouldn't have fancied the ladies in the bakery now so perhaps it is just that mams have got fitter. I have been on the facespace and checked a few of them out and they are not as aesthetically pleasing as you might like. You'd have to be really drunk. And definitely one of them would scrape your dick when she's sucking you off. It's a real problem that. I don't know if there's a technique which you learn about where they don't scrape your dick but it should be talked about. I don't fink you should suffer in silence. I don't fink you should sit there and take the pain. You should go, 'Oi, you dingbat, it's hurting!'

157

BRADBURY BAKERY
ESTD 1985

Pupil: Keith Lemon
Dates: 14 July – 25 July
Workplace: Bradbury Bakery

Keith's baking skills were nothing to shout about. He managed basic sandwich making. He wasn't happy about wearing a hairnet which is required. All in all, Keith is pleasant and I'm sure if it's something he is interested in then he will excel. Not sure working at a bakery is for him though. If Keith has any interest in doing more work experience here in the future we'd be happy to take him back but not just on his charm alone. He'd have to be more committed. The girl from t'other school doing work experience at the same time as Keith was a perfect example of what we'd expect if Keith was to return. She was also wanted to ask if she could have Keith's telephone number. I said I would ask.

Yours sincerely

Lynne Patrick

little keith lemon

WISPA, BRAD PITT, JOHNNY DEPP AND TERRY

For my fourteenth birthday, me mam bought me a rabbit. We called it Wispa – named after the chocolate bar. I had transfer stickers on the outside of the hutch and I used to change its name every week. I changed it to Brad Pitt once and it were also Johnny Depp the following week. And then we settled on Terry. And then a fox got hold of it and wrecked it's back legs. It were a traumatic time and I learnt about the fragility of life. I had to hit it on the back of the head with a spade to put it out of its misery. It were terrible. I remember crying. It were like a man test, I felt like I were in a live version of the film *Watership Down*. It did used to bite me though. And it did shit loads which I had to clean out so I weren't sad to see the back of that. I fink me mam were trying to teach us the responsibility of looking after somet.

After that, she arranged for me to go and look after an old man called Tony. At the time I thought he were about 200 years old but he were probably about 75. Me mam said that after his wife had died he got lonely so he could do with a young visitor to cheer him up. I used to take me gran's betamax and we'd watch stuff, but one day he started having a wank so I had to leave.

That were too much even if he were lonely. I fink he were a bit mad. I tried going to see old ladies instead and this one old lady, Florence, she got a bit friendly too. I don't know what it was about them! 'Oooo in't your hair all shiny. What do you put on it?' she used to say. I used to put Brylcreem on it but, I don't fink that were the point. I knew she wanted somet more from me and I remember finking 'I don't even fancy mam's, so when am I gonna fancy grandmas? What age do I have to be before I fancy a grandma?' I fink the age difference was just a bit too much.

WHO NEEDS PORN WHEN YOU'VE GOT LADS' MAGS?

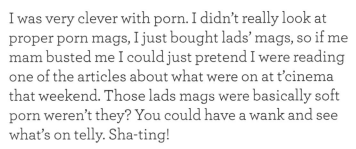

I was very clever with porn. I didn't really look at proper porn mags, I just bought lads' mags, so if me mam busted me I could just pretend I were reading one of the articles about what were on at t'cinema that weekend. Those lads mags were basically soft porn weren't they? You could have a wank and see what's on telly. Sha-ting!

I remember *Loaded* used to feature Liz Hurley a lot and she were right fit so I used to pump fist to that one all the time.

Another reason why I din't need any pornos of me own were that Pisshole used to have an old suitcase under his bed which were rammed full of pornos. We used to both have a torch in our hands so we could see the ladies and then we'd just bash off in the dark. If the batteries ran out, you'd have to wait until your eyes adjusted to the dark so you could see the breasts. Pisshole were on one side of the room and I were on t'other side of the room. It were like we were having a three-way affair with the suitcase. I guess looking back at it now it were a bit weird that we were both in the same room, knowing the other one was bashing one out, but at the time that were pretty normal. It were a bonding experience.

It were the same with watching porn on telly – it weren't somet you necessarily did by yerself. It wasn't a singular thing, we all used to watch it together. We used to go over to Mick's house and all watch it together. It would be like this:
'Has yer dad got any pornos?'
'Yeah.'
'Right, we're coming over'.

And that was their reputation made, someone would always be famous for being the one with the pornos and in our little group it were Mick. Mick's dad had loads of videos so we used to hang out there quite

a lot and watch 'em. We'd wait until the parents went out and we'd all sit there with pillows over our laps hiding our stiffies.

But porn were different back then. We didn't have Brazilians back then so everyone had a hairier bush. In the porn mags when I were growing up, the women had as much hair on their minge as they have on their head, din't they? You could place a table tennis ball on it, couldn't you? It would just sit there. It was literally like a pyramid of pubes.

Porn were basically the next step up from Wonder Woman. You started with Wonder Woman and then a year or so later, you were watching porn in Mick's sitting room. Wonder Woman looked ace though, din't she? I remember finking 'I wonder what she looks like in between the change where she is taking her normal clothes off and changing into her Wonder Woman clothes because those bumps on front look magnificent!' and that were the signal. You're ready for porn, son. She's got a wonderful chest Belinda Carter. She were one of me early crushes.

I have never had a wet dream but if I did I bet it would have been about Wonder Woman. I don't understand wet dreams though. Like every other man, I used to wake up in the morning with a hard on but I never had a wet dream. I remember waking up on the number 42 bus and having a hard on and not being able to get off the bus. I had to walk all the way back from top of hill to get back to me house while I waited for it to subside. Again, I used to fink about algebra to take my mind off it and turn me stiffy into a flop-on. Takes the pressure out of it. When you are a teenager you are basically walking coathangers.

little keith lemon

OH MY GOD.

Me mam just walked
in on me having a
wank.
OH MY GOD

I am never going
to wank again?

We both just pretended
it didn't happen
But it did.

Oh my god.

I've got to go downstairs
now cos me tea's ready

ME MATES FROM SHEFFIELD

I were about fourteen when I first met Gino, that's why I don't understand why he denies his Sheffield roots. Sheffield's not far from Leeds and we used to go Meadowhall shopping centre and hang out there. One time when we were there, we were messing around on our BMXs and Gino was there and was pulling a few tricks so we adopted him into our gang for a bit. He had a beard, which were a bit weird as he were only fifteen. He looked a bit like he was from *Withnail & I*, you know, like he stunk with a long coat on. When ITV got his hands on him they definitely did a makeover because he looked a bit like a tramp when I met him. He was very good at doing an Italian accent, it were like his party tricky. I'm not sure why he was called Gino. Perhaps it wasn't his real name? It sounds exotic though, don't it? But it is has worked out for him. He stays in character longer than anyone I have ever known. He is a lovely fella. He is very open sexually. He was a bit of a wild child. His Italian accent was a bit like me bandage. It were his fing. I fink that is how he got ladies actually.

He were, and still is, a right charmer. You had to keep him away from me mam. Me mam liked all me friends. She knew some of them were a bit cheeky and naughty but there were no malice there. They were a right nice bunch. They weren't drug dealers or owt, just cheeky buggers, but Gino always knew how to smooth talk his way into her heart. He even said he liked her pancakes. Gino's been on *Juice* loads of times now. Everyone loves him on it. With his Italian impersonation he can get away with saying things that normal people can't say as it would be too rude. The funniest time was when he was referring to Fearne's humungous nostrils and he said 'I bet she can suck like fuck'. I pissed meself laughing.

Dermot O'Leary was in our gang when we were at school, too. He was always very stylish. Not to the extreme, though. I fink he's subtle with it. I'm more showbiz with it, more flamboyancy. Dermot lets his bulge do the talking these days. Good old Dermot. It is funny because he had a small penis at school. He's a top bloke. Good on him! At school, one of me mates said that the more you wank, the bigger your tallywhacker gets. I remember he said, 'Fink about it. If you're just pulling it all t'time, it's gonna grow, innit?' Makes sense. Science.

THE
SEVEN-A-DAY WALL

There were a rumour going round school that you'd go blind if you wank too much. Once I started wanking I wanked religiously all day and night, all t'time. Especially in school holidays. You'd wank like a lunatic. I developed a clever way of getting round the blindness though. There were a parade of shops at the bottom of our road and we used to climb up the lamppost to get a cheapy. Fun, and I could still have the use of me eyes! Before I knew it was a sex thing, I thought it was because I'm higher up and it was summat to do with the atmosphere that's giving me willy a tingle! You'd climb up and you'd see who can climb up and not do a piss. Ya know, spunk up!

But by the time we were fifteen we had our fake IDs ready to go and we started to work out which pubs would let us in so there were less time locked in our bedroom or up the lamppost. It weren't much of an issue for me as my moustache gave me an air of maturity beyond me years but for some of me mates, it were a bit more tricky. But with pubs came a whole new breeding ground. I met a girl who worked behind the bar in a pub once and she were an animal. I can remember saying to her, 'can I have two pints of lager and your phone number please?' And she said, 'yeah.' Ooosh! Simple as peas.

Been at home all day. Mam's at work. Fink our Greg is out making daisy chains or somet. Always doing girly fings. I've had 6 wanks already today. One over Kylie Minogue, one over Betty Boo - not the cartoon, the singer. Can't wank over cartoons not even Jessica Rabbit. If she was real yeah, but I aint wanking over a drawing. Oddly enough I had a wank over Anthea Turner. One over me next door neighbour, then I did Patsy Kensit in't back doors. I'm now

gonna have a frankenstein wank. All those women merged into one super woman. That'll be number seven! I'll probably hit the wank wall and faint. Wish me luck. Speaking of superwoman, I'm gonna put her in there too! Helen Slater she is fit. OOoosh!

First time at me house, she just took me hand and took me up to me bedroom and then she just ripped me trousers off. I thought, 'eh? No, don't I do the moves?' And then on the weekend she came over again and we had a full day session and of course because you're a teenager you just never know when you're gonna get some sex again, do you, so you just spend all day having sex. Couldn't do that now. I couldn't be bothered. All day? I fink me knob would hurt. But when you're a kid, you might never get sex for a year so you have to take all you can get when you can get it.

Anywhere, it din't last too long as her brothers din't like me. It were like a modern-day, gritty Romeo and Juliet. The hassle of it wasn't worth it. I thought she was pretty and that but I weren't besotted by her so when her brothers started getting lairy I just thought, I can't be bothered getting chased.

There was another girl I was seeing at the same time anywhere so it were getting a bit complex trying to balance the two. I met her in t'hospital as she was in the hospital bed next to me mam when me mam was having her knee looked at. She looked like Patsy Kensit – super bang. I remember I asked her whether she liked sharks and she was perplexed enough to want to find out more. I have always been good at asking people questions and it keeps the conversation flowing which is what ladies like. To talk. A lot.

Do you like sharks?
Can you body pop?
What is your favourite type of dinosaur?
I like your shoes, are they la bootins?
What is your name?

174

That sort of thing. But it's a great place to chat up birds – the hospital. People are often emotional wrecks when they're in there and are looking for guidance. They're like little Bambis on ice. Again, persistence is key. And if they are hooked up to a drip there ain't nowhere for them to go so they'll say they'll go on a date with yer just to shut you up for a bit. Plus, if they look fit when they're in hospital – no make-up or tan – then they are gonna look super bang when they get out of the place.

175

little keith lemon

little keith lemon

ME BIRD BECKY

But even though I were riding a lady wave, me main significant major relationship of me teenage years was with Becky Ramsey, when I were fifteen. I met her at the local youth club. We went out for about six months, which is a long time, in't it? Six months is a long time when you're fifteen. She wanked me off in t'back of car, it was so romantic. She had sort of dirty blonde hair. Not like as blonde as me but maybe as blonde as Mel Blatt from All Saints. She was a pretty girl, a bit taller than me and not much in the way of bangers.

She were at the bus stop on the way home from the local youth club. I said, 'Will you go out with me?'. She said 'No'. 'Will you go out with me?' 'No.' I knew she were gonna give in if I kept asking, so I kept at it. I got the 83 bus home with her and we sat on t'back seats obviously, still making her laugh and whatever else. And then, just before I got to the door to get off at my stop she said, 'yeah, alright then', and I snogged her there and then. I came away with her phone number in me hand.

Sometimes I used chat-up lines but you don't always need 'em. In this pacific case, it just took a bit of persistence and charm. But when that doesn't work, see over the page for some of me favourite lines:

I know milk does a body good, but DAMN... how much have you been drinking? I'd love to see you gargle it. I hope you know CPR cos you take me breath away. You can give me t'kiss of life if you like and stick yer tongue in.

Do you eat Frosties because you're bringing out the tiger in me? You look greeeaaaat! I'd love to have it off with yer.

I used to write her poems. Girls go mad for that sort of stuff. I can remember seeing some programme about poetry and it said that poems didn't have to rhyme. But it came straight from the heart! I wrote love letters too. I was big on love letters, I was, always writing love letters to Miss Birdmuff, to Angela, and to Becky. And cos I was good at drawing I would always draw a little picture of them in a different scenario. I'd often turn them into sort of fantasy characters and give 'em big shotguns. Imagine a beautiful girl holding Rambo's gun. How ace is that!

Becky, you are
stupid fit.
I'd let you kick
the crap out of me.

ROSES ARE RED
VIOLETS ARE BLUE
WHAT'S THE DILIO ?
WANNA GO SWIMMING ?

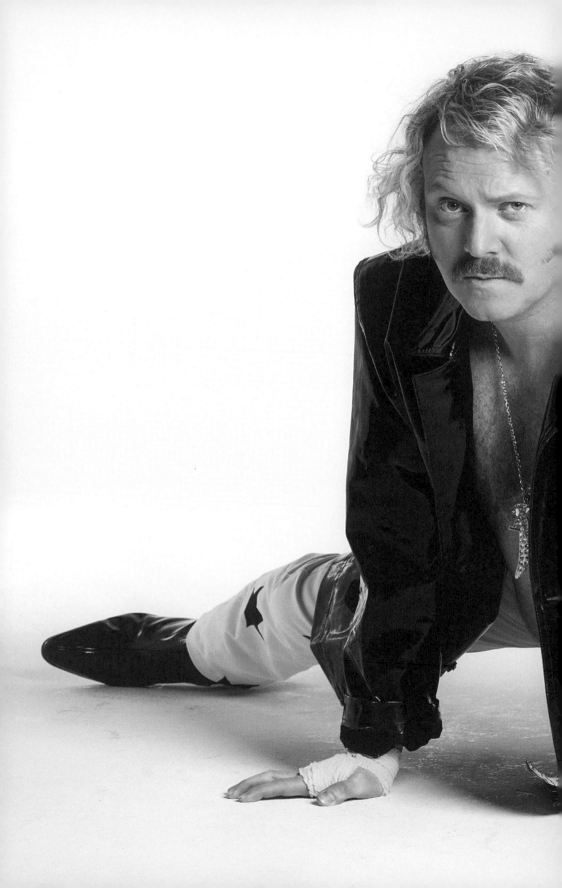

THE ART OF SEDUCTION

I remember the first time I buffed her. It were amazing. We had been watching *Basic Instinct* and had a nice bottle of Bianco that I bought from Wilkinson to get us in t'mood. I started to shove me fingers in Becky's mouth just like Michael Douglas does to Sharon Stone and I could tell she were getting turned on. I'd cleaned me hands especially as I'd had a doner kebab on the way over. I started to whisper sweet nothings in her ear. I can't remember exactly what I said but it would of being somet like: 'I'm as stiff as a brick for you. I want to sex you up, down, around and all over your god damn sexy body' or 'Would you like me to kiss your bangers on t'end? Not near the end but right on bloody end!' or as me mate Paddy might say, 'Let the tash see the gash.' She were going wild for it. I could see she were undressing me with her eyes.

As we were at her mam's house, we needed to find somewhere that her mam weren't going to come in offering us a cup of tea so we went to the car, which were parked in the garage. We put the back seats down to make it comfortable and we found an old sleeping bag that her brother had taken to scout camp the week before. She said it were perfect. I am a very giving lover and I always fink about the woman. Miss Birdmuff taught me that. I made sure that Becky had her fun before I blew me beans. What I normally do is fink about trivial things while me lady is having a great time and when she's had that great time and she's been up the hill and back down again, then I can start finking about what I'm doing. But I'll always try to give her one first. I normally fink about algebra. How can numbers equal letters? Eh? That doesn't make any sense! It keeps you going for another minute or two. It got right steamy in that car, it were like that scene from *Titanic*.

I remember bringing Becky home and introducing her to me mam for the first time. Me mam's inherently very nice and always very nice to every girl that I brought back. Sometimes she liked them more than I did and were quite saddened if I split up with them. I got over it quicker than she did! But she always liked Becky so when things had run their natural course, me mam was right sad. I don't fink I ever cried about it. I were too much of a man to cry. I still don't cry very easily these days. I remember when Rylan came on to *Celebrity Juice* and we played Keith vs Rylan to see who could push out a tear first. We looked at all this sad stuff, like a picture of Gary the dog RIP and I still couldn't push out a tear. Rylan won that one hands down. Rylan lost it after that. He were crying out for Gary and Nicole.

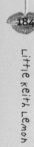

little keith lemon

Me new ~~resoltion~~ resolution for
this year is to stop wanking
so much. Seven a day is
insane. When you hit the
wall - the seven wall - and it
is just smoke coming out of-
t'end, you're got to stop.
Will aim for five a day

See, I were ahead of me
time on the five a day thing -
everyone talks about it now.
Perhaps I should be prime minisher?

ON AGAIN, OFF AGAIN

Most of me relationships had the same cycle. You stand around with yer mates on a street corner drinking warm beer out of a can wishing you had a bird. You eventually persuade one to go out with you. It gets all intense and you don't see your mates for a bit. Then you see your mates and you fink, 'oh fuck, I miss me mates. I don't want a girlfriend. I want to stand on t'street corner with me mates praying that I had a girlfriend.' So you go all boring until they split up with you. Then you see 'em somewhere, you might see 'em with another guy or whatever, and you go, 'fuck, I liked her.' Then you'd try going back out with her and she did the 'no, no, no,' thing and then said 'ok'. Me and Becky went round like that for years.

It were normally Becky that would start fancying me again. One time she actually created someone that I was supposed to be jealous of and a mate told me. Girls are clever, aren't they? A mate told me that she weren't seeing anyone. I confronted her about it and said 'I know you're not seeing anyone, you're just making it up to make me jealous, but I'm not jealous. You fucking wanker!' I fink she were a bit surprised by me language but I thought she were a fucking loon! As an adult I fink these things happen all the time but back then I thought she were mad.

But a couple of months later we were at it again, this time in the loos of a nightclub. 'Oh hi . . . Yeah, oh, nice to see you ... who are you with?' 'Oh, me mates'. And then she was feeling me leg under t'table. I had baggy chinos on so I had to stay sitting down for a while until all me happiness had gone. And then she said, 'do you wanna go for a bit in t'toilets?' We went to girls' toilets and I remember her saying, 'harder, harder, faster' and I thought I can't go any harder or faster, this is as fast as I go. How fast are you supposed to go? In the girls' loos! I didn't know how fast I was supposed to go. I thought if I go any faster I'm gonna look silly. Nowadays, I take it nice and slow. Whisper sweet nothings in her ear, right breathy like 'you make me wobbly like jelly, oooosh'. It does the trick. Anywhere, I didn't blow me beans because someone came in t'toilet. It's a bit like having a poo. I weren't finking 'Oh, this is a beautiful moment.' It was all practicalities. Do this, get over with this and then tell me mates. And I remember me balls killing me afterwards.

But then, a few months later someone said, 'did you shag Becky?' When I said that I had indeed shagged Becky, they said I didn't. Now, I don't know the Laws of Shagging but I reckon if penis is in vagina, it counts. Otherwise it would be like saying when a lady fakes an organism, they haven't actually done it.

I wasn't worried about getting her pregnant as I used to pull out just in time. Finking about it perhaps that should be one of my top five main primary skills – pulling out on time. I've got good willpower. No one's ever come forward saying, 'Keith this is your baby.' Well, a few have but I can't remember. Me and Becky had sex many times at school but she went out with a lot of people and so did I.

little keith lemon

You're confused, aren't you, when you're a kid. Mates or muff? Muff or mates? You all want muff but you don't want to leave your little gang. If you've got a girlfriend, all yer mates will call you a poof. You puff! It doesn't make sense really. How can I be a puff if I've got a girlfriend?

But despite all of the activity I were getting, I've never actually fallen in love. I thought I did, but I wouldn't be able to get over it so easy if she really were the one. I've seen *The Notebook* and other films and it takes 'em ages and their soul's all broken up and they can't operate, can they? But when I've broken up I go, 'stupid witch. Fuck it!' And then I get on with life, so I can't have been in love.

little keith lemon

VALENTINE'S DAY

I always used to make an effort on Valentine's Day
– girls love it. This is one of the Valentine's Day cards
I sent to Becky.

But even if I weren't seeing one bird in particular at
the time, I would make sure I sparkled a little bit of the
Lemon love out there. Just to cheer a few girls up. It's
only fair. Sometimes I would send a special mysterious
message and other times I thought it were best just to
cut to the chase: 'I fucking fancy you, it's Keith, by the
way. Will you go out with me?'

Those were the words. I must have said that sentence
a million times to different women over the years.
'Will you go out with me?' 'No.' 'Go on.' 'No.' 'Go on.'
'No.' 'Go on.' 'Alright.' 'Ace.'

That was me strategy. Be persistent. Even today if I talk
to someone who finks that they're out of my league or
whatever, I'll say to them:
'I could pull you if I wanted to.'
And they'd say, 'no you can't cos I wouldn't go out
with you.'
'Yeah, you would.'
'No, I wouldn't.'
'Look, if I wanted to I would.'

Persistence. Until you get the police phoning you
asking you to leave her alone, just keep asking the
question. That's never happened to me as I would have

Valentine

I'm head over heels...

hooked them in by then. But I always fink guys are too quick just to give up. But if there is one thing I have learnt it is that the ladies like the chase. Especially when they're a bit older. They don't really care what you look like, you can just go at it until they say yeah. They'll be bored one day, won't have anything to do on a weekend and just say 'oh fuck it, how bad is it gonna be?' and then that's when you do your work. When you take her out, that's when the work kicks in. You use every trick. Every trick. And if you don't know what the tricks are let me tell you what the tricks are. Actually, I'm not gonna tell yer, you have to get me other book – *The Rules: 69 Rules for Being a Success*. Go and buy that yer cheapskate. Did yer fink I were just going to repeat the same stuff over and over? Dingbat.

In my case, the hardest fing weren't actually getting someone to go out with yer, it were the splitting up with someone. I'm hard on t'outside and soft on t'inside you see. I always felt really guilty about it so what I would do when I was a kid was I'd just pretend to be fucking boring. Boring. And stop laying on all the compliments. Stop all that being nice stuff, go a bit quiet. Eventually, they will ask 'Is there summat wrong?' 'No.' It won't take long before they come back to you saying 'I don't fink it's gonna work out.' Job done. And you have done your bit for empowering women. All round winner.

One of me mates, Gay Simon, now he actually were a puff. He din't tell us at the time but he were always the one saying you were a puff if you had a girlfriend. I remember when he first told us, we were at a house party in Beeston. We were only going to the party because Frank fancied this girl and she were gonna be there. It was in a house that looked a bit like a squat. I din't know anyone there but I were feeling pretty merry as I'd had a few jars by this point. Frank had come round to ours and we'd drunk four cans of Gold Label barley wine. The first mouthful tastes like the devil having a piss in your mouth, but then you have another one and then another one and then you can't taste anyfing.

We'd have four of them because we had no money and then we'd go out and spend about a fiver. Anyway, at the party, I can remember impressing some of the girls when I drew pictures of them with these coloured soaps I found in t' bathroom. I were like Neil Buchanan on *Art Attack*. Frank were getting it on with the bird he fancied so I ended up chatting to her mate who was less aesthetically pleasing, and Gay Simon came over, a few cans down and just came out with it. Everyone kept having these backflashes to times we had spent together and finking 'was he looking at me then?' 'Did he fancy me?' 'Was he trying to get his end away after football?' and all that. He did ask me how I felt about him being gay. I wasn't fucking bothered. I said to him, 'I live with a gay, don't I, so it don't bother me if you suck dicks or get your arsehole poked or bum men or jizz in the face.' I like all kinds ... black, white, pink, yellow, lesbicans, pillow-biters. I don't get irate about it.

little keith lemon

RHINO JEANS

Other than a few Saturday jobs and me paper round from Bottom Shop, me first step on the entrepreneurial ladder were selling Rhino jeans on Leeds Market. I were saving up to get me mam a new pair of teeth. She needed 'em. Her teeth looked like a dirty picket fence in her mouth so I thought after all the years that she had been looking after me and Greg, it would be nice to give her a little somet back. The jeans were a bit dodgy though. I don't know where they came from. A lad that I knew, he had a whole pile of these jeans and they were rejects, factory seconds, so they'd all have a belt loop missing or they wouldn't have any pockets. The most common problem were that one leg would be fatter than t'other. We basically bought them, got a few labels printed saying RHINO JEANS, stuck 'em on and sold 'em on.

I saw a gap in the market – Branson, see? – and thought I could fill it. I knew from experience that jeans got a lot of wear and tear around the crown jewels area and the material can get worn out. I'm not sure if it were just because I had a big cock and balls but it were always worn out down there for me. So Rhino jeans were made out of much tougher material – like a rhino's skin – so that those who are well-endowed could wear them without fear of their tallywhacker flopping out.

People would bring them back and say 'oi, Keith, one leg is bigger than t'other' but I used to say, 'yeah, but you are encapsulating both ragamuffin and emo style in one go so everyone will like you in those jeans, won't they?' I have always been a good salesman me. I don't

little keith lemon

fink the emo look had even been invented back then and now it's caught on. I invented that. The other solution I had was that you could get a skateboard to make one leg more muscly than t'other and then it would pad out the wider leg. Sorted. I've still got a couple of boxes of them for old times sake.

I got good banter from working on the market. You have to shout stuff and make people want to come and look at your stall rather than anyone else's.

'COME AND GET YOUR JEANS, £11.60 FOR YOUR JEANS. RIGHT GOODUNS. LIKE LEVI'S BUT NOT AS GOOD AS LEVI'S.'

We sold them on Leeds Market, next to the stall that sold chickens. I fancied the girl on the next stall, Donna, and I had a little dabble with her as well. She used to give me a bit of breast for free.

Harlington High

Careers Assessment
Student: Keith Lemon
Class: 5B

Keith Lemon seems to either have a very positive attitude of his own future or is living in a fantasy world. Has no interest in further education which is a shame as I don't feel academically he is at the same level as his fellow students.

He is convinced he has work lined up straight from school in the form of his own business? Apparently he has a stall on Leeds Market selling denim jeans. Not sure if this is true and I very much doubt this will lead to anything with any kind of longevity. But he seems very confident that he knows what he is doing. We did discuss other options in case things don't go to plan but again, he seems determined and already has his mind set.

He is very different to the rest of the students, whatever the future holds I'm sure his flamboyant dress sense and interesting use of the English language will get him noticed somewhere and thus dictate his path.

Dains

Mr Dains
Careers Officer

Harlington High
Form teacher's report
Student's name: Keith Lemon
Class: 5B

Student's strengths

Keith is very good at communicating with the class
even though sometimes he doesn't seem to understand
exactly what it is he's trying to communicate. He
does need to concentrate more in class. It's good that
he enjoys school but sometimes he enjoys it too much.
If he put as much effort into his actual schoolwork
as he does with the highly detailed sexy drawings
he does in the back of his exercise books, he'll pass
his GCSEs with flying colours. A lot of the time when
our students struggle academically they excel in
other areas. Unfortunately Keith doesn't. He is good
at talking and drawing sexy pictures. I'm not really
sure what the future holds for him.

What can the student do to improve?

As above, if he could pay more attention in class,
I think he has the potential to be a satisfactory
student. It would also help if he attended class
a bit more.

Harlington High
Form teacher's report
Student's name: Keith Lemon
Class: 5B

Overall

Keith is a kind-hearted young man with a mind of his
own. He doesn't like to listen and although he's not
completely disruptive to class, he doesn't make it easy
for any of our tutors either. Our female tutors, in
particular, report that he seems to show off in their
presence and is unable to concentrate. Saying that,
if Keith knuckled down and didn't bask in the glory of
being the class clown, he could do better. The one area
where he really excels is art, especially when it comes
to the female form.

LAST DAYS AT SCHOOL

Our last week at school was really fun. We had all finished our exams and hadn't yet had our results so we could just mess about. I was excited cos as much as I enjoyed school whilst I was there, it seemed like the start of adulthood. Our Greg went on t'further education. He's got a lot of qualifications. I don't know what for. It's like he just likes collecting degrees. I'm sure he'll do somet really good one day. He's got a good job now I fink but I don't know what he does. Somet with t'ozone layer I fink. I din't know we still had one. Nobody talks about it anymore do they? They always use to go on about it on John Craven's *Newsround* don't they, saying we're gonna fuck it up if we use hairspray. It must've healed.

I remember the day we got our exam results. I'm not gonna embarrass meself and tell ya what I came out with but the brainiest kid in't school only came out with four GSCEs. And he was brainy as fuck. He were like a scientist, he could've built a time machine that bastard. I fink the marking system must've been defunked back then. Fink it was only the second yeah or so that they'd being doing GSCEs. It don't matter, I've never needed 'em anyway. That's not to say anyone young that's reading these should just fuck about at school and come out with nowt though. Anywhere, I cun't wait t'get a proper job and have some proper money. I wan't sad that I wasn't gonna see me mates again cos I never thought that were gonna be t'case.

It's only now that I miss 'em. Cos I don't see 'em as much now. But we're all still in touch.

When I left school they din't have one of those Yearbook fings like they have in American teen movies, but I always liked the idea of one. So over the page is me virtual Yearbook – what might've been if they had've been.

KEITH LEMON YEAR BOOK 1992

Well, what a great time we had! We din't learn too much. But we had fun and copped a feel of some of the birds from the school opposite. Sometimes, whilst learning nowt and looking at the girls playing netball in t'other school outta the window, I wished that our school was mixed. But I'm sure I'd be a dad by now if that were the case so maybe it was a blessing. Maybe I am a dad. I've had a few experience where me welly has ripped while I've been paddling but always prideded meself on having the ability to pull out at the right time.

Most of us will probably go on to have boring jobs but one day I'm probably gonna have me own company and you'll go on Facebook and tell people ya went to school with me. I'll message ya back and I'll say 'yeah I went t'school with ya and din't we have a great time', whilst all along I'll be finking 'cor, you've put some timber on.' By now I'm probably the boss of Securipole which is gonna revolutionise urban car protection in a way than equals what Playstation did to the games console or what the crab stick did to the fish food industry. Good luck t'all I went t'school with, I hope ya wife is fit and you've got a good job. Remember if ya can dream it, ya can lie about.

PS. *Facebook doesn't exist yet but if ya don't know what it is, let me tell you what it is, is a social network fing where ya can look up ya old birds and see if they're still fit or turned fat.*

Cheers!
Keith Lemon

THE LEEDS BOYS GO TO KAVOS!

After me GCSEs, I were keen to get out into t'world and start making a name for meself. But first things first, we were gonna go on our first proper lads' holiday. To Kavos. Ay up Kavos! The Leeds boys are in town! We were staying in this mint hotel by the beach. Belly just kept going round getting photographs of him with random lasses in bikinis. But the only people he were showing these photographs to were us and we knew that he hadn't shagged any of 'em. You can't go, 'look, shagged her on holiday... shagged her on holiday...' We were with you! You can't just get a picture. I fink it were for his wankboard at home.

I went on holiday with Belly again recently and he's still doing the same thing! Taking photographs of fings. We got kicked out of a nightclub for him taking photographs of girls cos it was a bit more upmarket nightclub and they got a beef on about it. They kicked us out. We din't know we were getting kicked out at the time. They just said, 'gentleman, would you like to come over here.' We thought we were getting VIP treatment and then we looked back, and we're outside.

Anywhere, it were a wicked holiday. It were ace. It was sunny all the time. And all the women are pissed. It were incredible. We went on one of those paragliding things that hurts your middle bits.

I didn't go on a banana boat and that's one of me biggest regrets in life that I didn't go on a banana boat that holiday. I don't know what I were finking. You get to straddle girls in their bikinis and act the hero when they get thrown in. I was made for it! I remember we went on a boat trip to some other part of the island with the old town and it was shit. 'I fink we should go to old town . . .' 'Really?' 'Yeah,' 'Ok.' But it's old. It's shit.

I can remember when we first got there, we went out too early. We went out at about six o'clock, cos we were so excited. Nobody was out! We realised on about the third night that no one goes out till about 10, by which point we were already a bottle of Malibu down. We were like, 'hey, it's a bit dead, innit?' And by the time it got busy we were all so drunk and couldn't even walk. It were hard because we were used to drinking before you go out so it's a cheaper night, innit?

The only problem for me were that I were going out with Becky at the time. Now you don't want to go on a holiday like that and have a girlfriend. The two things just don't go together. I mean, I did all the right stuff. I even sent her a postcard:

I'll have to tell you what it said because you can't see what it said now that I've stuck it in:

Dear Becky

Having a shit time in Kavos. Got asked to partake in
a 3some with Frank. But said no. These two other girls
wanted me to have a 3some and I said no. The idea
of a threesome makes me sick unless it were two of
you. Can't wait to see you. I hope you understand I only
came here to make Dave feel better because his dad
died. And now I am going to have to stay an extra week
to make him feel better. Sorry, this is the only postcard
I could find.

Love you.

Love Keith.

I was having such a great time, I stayed an extra week.
Dave's dad isn't dead. He were off work and slipped
a disc. It would've broke her heart if I had told her
though and I were too young for this type of
commitment. And at least I had sent her a postcard.
To be honest, I were excited to see if the postcard even
got to her. Whenever I have posted somet from abroad,
I always fink, 'it's never gonna get there' and when it
does you can't believe it can you! I get lost in the
airport so how does it get there?

YOU'VE GOT TO HAVE A THREESOME

Anywhere, back to Kavos. You've got to have had a threesome in life, haven't yer? It's one of those boxes you've just got to tick. I mean, only just to tell your mates. Obviously, if you were mature enough you wouldn't do it because you wouldn't rush into somet you didn't necessarily want to do, but you *are* rushing because you don't want to be left behind. If someone else has done summat you don't want to be left behind, so you all want to fuck and suck and lick and whatever else just so you can say you've done it and know what people are talking about when they give it all the chat at school.

It did feel a bit weird having sex with Frank there, especially when your knob touches his. More recently, I've done it with two girls, which is better. But when your knob touches another man's knob by accident, it is like you are in a Willliam Shatner nightmare, it is like the whole world goes wonky and wobbly. You can get an instant flop on. Like two swords moving around and then there is an instant reaction when another man's knob touches yours and it goes flaccid and it is over. It is very similar to using a public toilet. You don't really enjoy the woman as much as you are looking at the ceiling most of the time as you don't want to be looking into the other guy's eyes. But I were glad to have ticked the box.

One box I have never ticked is having me arsehole licked. I have never had my arsehole licked and I have never licked anyone else's arsehole. I am a bit scared. What if she has a smelly bum? What if she is super fit and she has a smelly bum, you'd go off her wouldn't you? I remember when Becky tried to stick her finger up me arse. It were the time when you heard rumours of sexual exploits and you'd try everything out just to say you'd done it but she tried to stick her finger up there and I could have snapped her finger off. 'Eh? What are you doing? That is a deposit box only. I don't need to go up there, so you don't need to either. It is a drop-off zone, you can't put money into it, you just get money out of it.'

I find quite a few of me fans want to stick their fingers up me arse. The older the fans, the dirtier they are. They are always trying to get their fingers up there, it's weird. I don't know what it is this obsession with arseholes. I know that an arse looks right nice from a distance but when you get up close, all you can see is this star, a tight little star. Further back, an arse is nice but close up it is like a brown space door.

⌄⌄ SECURIPOLE ⌄⌄

After I got back from Kavos, I knew I had to find meself a job. Me experience on the market had taught me that my skills would be best utilised as a businessman. I had a couple of other options at the time. Because of me breakdancing skills, I had got meself noticed on dance floors across Leeds. Me moves were basically a mating call. I sometimes used to mix it up a bit and do a bit of Russian Cossack dancing. I fink the girls were impressed by my athletic ability. You have to be careful though because your legs ache like bastards the next day. The other option is to just do a body shake. The closer you get to the girl, the sexier it is. I've copped off with many girls like this.

Anywhere, as I were saying, me dancing was getting me noticed across Leeds and further afield and I was asked to take part in an audition for a new pop group. When I got there, I was standing in front of Steps. They were looking for an extra member and they thought I were the man for the part. I wowed them with me dancing and I could sing right good too. They were desperate for me to be a part of the group but I didn't want to wear that yellow outfit – I'd look like a fisherman. So I turned it down.

The only thing that made me fink twice were that Claire. She were a right one. She has that same bunny rabbit nose that Emma Bunton has. Dead cute.

But as I say, I discovered I wanted to be a businessman so I set up Securipole. I found a load of poles in a skip. I don't fink that is stealing, I just thought 'I will have

Be a robbing bastards bone of contention with a 'Securipole' right now!

Our prices range from high to low. So don't worry. Call us now for a FREE! Quotation on

0113 777 777 8900000

There is almost no obligation and before you know your car could be being protected with a pole.

Choose from a variety of styles and prices from just a few of our we recommended models below. Spoil yourself it's my treat!

Securipole Bruce Lee PPFWL - Orders 10 to 25 off (Reference #198)

Fold down parking post in yellow finish. Height 63cm.

Built-in top locking tubular key cylinder. Right tough and light on it's feet.

Special discount for orders of 10 to 25 off.

Price : £85.00 £99.88 Including VAT at 17.5%

Securipole 'Predator' (Reference #215)

Secured by fitting a suitable padlock through the locking pin which is engaged at the base of the post. This pole will kick the crap out of any unwanted visitors. Galvanised finish is to B5729. Supplied c/w black polypropylene weather cap.

Price : £136.83 £160.78 Including VAT at 17.5%

Securipole 'Terminator' (Reference #216)

Galvanised finish is to B5729. Supplied c/w black polypropylene weather cap. Socket flap closes flush to the ground. This mean mother has more aggression than a house brick in the hands drunken naughty man!

Price : £136.83 £160.78 Including VAT at 17.5%

Securipole

for every man!

Hello my name is Keith Lemon, owner of 'Securipole'.

Not deputy head, but full owner of the whole company. That's right I was so impressed with 'Securipole' I bought the company just like that man with the Remington thing. So why was I so impressed I hear you ask? Well, let me tell you if isn't obvious for you to see just be looking at the picture adjacent to this text. Many people don't like it when bastards thief their car,. That's right bastards! The only word that can be used to describe these low lives. To a man his car is his castle on wheel's, a house that can be moved from A to B. So he wants to protect that house. With a 'Securipole'! What 'Securipole is a two-foot reinforced aluminium shaft installed in the driveway. It's so easy to use even a woman or a disabled person can use it. You'll be able to sleep at night knowing your car is safe like an hamster or indeed a budgie in a cage, or any other family pet, because it might sound daft, but a car is also like a family pet. I believe in this product so much I have two erections. One in my back passage and one up my front. It doesn't take a genius or a clever scientist to know that your car is going to be safer with a pole in front of it.

SPECIFICATION:

Tubular posts with top caps. All products strong welded steel construction with a weatherproof galvanised finish.

Hinged posts: mounted on base plate. Hinged with facility for padlock to lock in either raised or lowered position. (Padlock not included) Either predrilled base plate with 4 holes for bolting to the ground (surface fixing) or base plate with extension piece for concreting into the ground (submerged fixing). Post height 900mm, Overall height 920mm, base plate size 150mm x 110mm. Also available in key lock versions details on request.

Removable posts: socket for concreting into the ground with removable post. Socket has hinged top cap to cover when post not in position, also provides facility for padlock

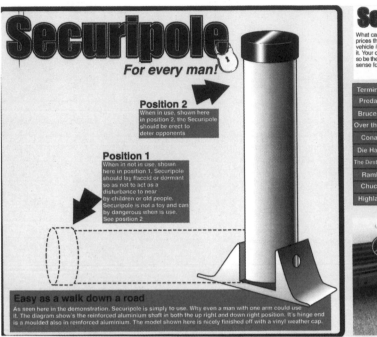
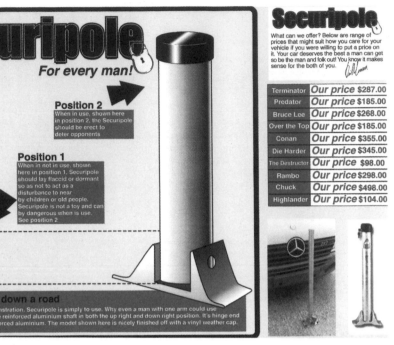
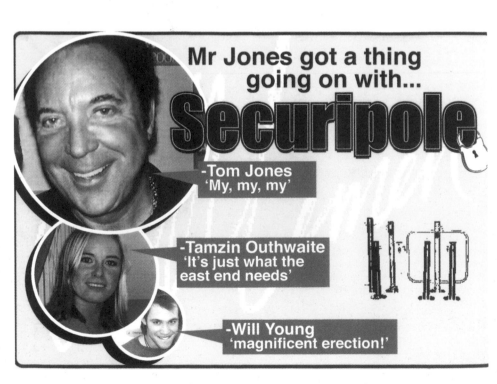

them, I will be able to sell them.' If you don't know what a Securipole is, let me tell you what it is. It is a two-foot reinforced aluminium shaft you can have installed in your driveway to prevent evil scum buggers from stealing your car, or your auto moto vehicle as scientists call them.

The skills I learnt on the market came in useful as selling anything on a market is quite similar to door-to-door selling, which is how I first started selling the Securipoles. Obviously, I didn't shout when I knocked on someone's door:

'Would you like to buy a Securipole? The finest Securipoles are here.'

You say it, but it is similar communication skills. I connect with people. The phone number was on the parking posts so that whenever people saw them and thought 'I need to get me one of those reinforced aluminium parking posts to protect my auto moto vehicle from being nicked by evil scum buggers' they could call us up and order one. That is marketing. I came up with the name Securipole which I thought were genius. They were poles that kept your car secure. Securipoles. I remember getting done by some sort of trading standards thing because my slogan was 'It is scientifically proven that gyppos like your car more than you do. Get a Securipole'. It doesn't rhyme, but that is why it made you fink more: 'You know what, I should watch out'. We take fings for granted, and we shouldn't.

SPLASHING THE CASH

It was nice to have some proper money and say to girls, 'I've got me own business.' I fink the ladies were always quite impressed when I handed them me business card with a wink. Better than writing your phone number on a cigarette paper, in't it? My card was one of the first cards to be made out of sperspex. I don't know if you remember that trend? Instead of a paper business card, for Securipole we had nice clear sperspex ones.

I didn't actually drive meself when I first started the business. I was selling security for your car but I didn't have a car meself. It din't take me long to save up enough cash to buy one though. Me first car was a red Escort. It was really eyecatching and a bit of a minge magnet.

Anyway, for me services to Securipole, I was awarded the Northern Business Man of the Year and that is when me business life as an entrepreneur all got a bit more interesting. I suppose winning Business Man of the Year at such a young age kind of confirmed I was special and having the initiative to sort meself out. I'm not working for someone. I'll set up me own shit and sell parking posts. You had to be nominated to enter the competition so I nominated meself. I don't fink people do that enough. Why not? All you have to do is enter yourself under a different name. So the Northern Business Man of the Year panel had a letter from Denzel Murgatroyd saying 'Keith Lemon's the best. His reinforced parking posts are beyond compare. He has grown his business one post at a time and he looks set to be the Richard Branson of the Leeds parking world.'

Then I had to go for an interview at Leeds Town Hall with a board of judges. I used half a bottle of the Paco Rabanne before that and put on me best linen suit. It did the trick and I cun't believe it when I won. I entered as a bit of a laugh. And I won! I won! I was on t'*Calendar* as well, which is the Leeds TV news. It were basically like going on *This Morning* with Holly and Phil, though not quite as good as there were no Holly and there were no Phil, who are two of me favourite people. Holly and her massive bangers. She's a lovely bird. Drinks like a tramp. Uncle Phil has still got it. His hair is silver but his pubes are as black as a raven's wing. I love it when he comes on *Juice*. The second time he were on it were one of our most-watched episodes of all time. He told us a story about one guest who came on to *This Morning* who showed him and Holly her minge all the way through t'interview. Ooooosh!

219

little keith lemon

Northern Business Man of the Year

PROUDLY PRESENTED TO

Keith Lemon

JOHN L. DOE, President

JANE DOE, Vice-President

little keith lemon

I weren't doing anything like that on *Calendar* but I guess they wanted a bit of totty in front of the camera so that must've helped. I even crossed paths with the late, great Richard Whiteley. What a hero! I were really excited because I thought I might get to meet Carol Vorderman as well. I like Carol Vorderman. She's saucy. She is bang tidy. After she saw me in me pants on *Loose Women* I sent her a text every day with me in me pants. Not me face, just my panted area. I stopped after seven days as you can have too much of a good thing, I fink. It's like blowjobs. They should only be granted as a treat.

What I find mad about Carol Vordeman is that she likes numbers. That woman likes maths. There's somet not right there. The only thing I remember about me maths lessons was the teacher saying, 'now bring down an extra nought.' I couldn't understand that concept of bringing a number down. 'What you on about? An extra nought? Where do I get that from?' And why is it cheating to use a calculator? It's like saying 'Did you write all that by hand with a pen?' 'No, I did it on the computer.' 'Well, you need to do it with a pen.' It's all bollocks. Sorry Carol.

To celebrate me being crowned Northern Business Man of the Year, me and a group of me mates went to Amsterdam. It's a right funny old place. Belly were in his element, walking up and down the red light district, looking at the ladies and taking photos. He couldn't afford to actually go in. He were a virgin so he were desperate to get laid. So we all put our hands in our pockets and bought him a treat. As we'd never been to Amsterdam before and none of us knew how long you're supposed to be with a prostitute or what

happens even, other than the obvious, we were waiting for ages and thought, effing hell, there's somet going on, there's somet wrong with him, what's going on? And then the lady came out and said 'your friend wants more time.' Cheeky bastard! I actually got so sick to death of sex. It cancelled itself out. In the end we just went to the pub. But you couldn't even get away from it in the pub! Right behind the bar, there were a huge telly showing a big tallywhacker coming out of a hole it shouldn't be coming out of and when I blinked all I could see was that wide-open hole. It were like when you have a photograph taken and you get a green dot in your eye every time you blink … all I could see was a wide open hole. I fink we were all ready to go home after that. We din't even have any space cakes!

little keith lemon

TWENTY-ONE AT LAST

I never thought I would make it to twenty-one.
I always thought I would get run over. I was too
carefree. I remember when I did make it to twenty-one
and I thought 'ace, now I can have arse sex.' But now
that I have had arse sex, I'm not sure it is that big a
deal. I know on *Celebrity Juice* I talk about smashing
a lady's back doors in but that's all bravado. I'm
quite a sensitive guy really. I just haven't found love
yet, but I'd like to. I'm not the dickhead I was when
I was younger, only when I'm pissed up. I'm probably
a good catch. I have many TVs and a soda stream!

When we were growing up, you had to do everything
and then tell your mates about it. It were like a tick box
thing. And I'm not talking about doing any number
ones or number twos on anyone, that's just gross and
dirty. 'I like you, can I do me toilet on you?' What's that
about? It's mental! Belly went out with a bird who was
in to that stuff but only in the bath so she could wash
it off afterwards! He weren't so sure about it but out
of manners he returned the favour. That's right
weird that.

Anywhere, now that I'm here and I've passed
the twenty-one mark, I have started to get a bit
philosophical about life. I fink me mates are proud
of what I've done. At school, they were obviously
really jealous of me as I was right good looking.
But you can't help it if you were born that way. It is
like that woman on *I'm a Celebrity Get Me Out of Here*,
Amy Willington. They all hated her because she was

F.A.F but I met her and she was right nice.
I'd let her kick the crap out of me.

Looking back I don't fink I'd have done anyfing
differently. Maybe I'd have timed it so that when
I met Fearne Cotton I'd have been single, and who
knows, instead of marrying Jesse Wood she may have
got lucky and married me. He's a lovely bloke though.
I'm so happy for her. I even cried at her wedding – I've
obviously been hanging out with our Greg too much.
Of course, there's been a few ladies out there that now
looking back I've thought maybe there was somefing
special there but I just din't realise it at the time. For
an example, I should have at least had a go on Kelly
Brook's bangers. She's another one that's gonna be
married soon, or she might already be by t' time this
comes out. Sometimes I worry I am just gonna be left
on't shelves. Ha, ha, ha do I fuck. I'm a right fanny
magnet at the moment!

Anyway if you can't be bothered to read the whole
book, here's a little summary of what I got up to.
Then you can just look at the pictures.

BIRTH TO TWO YEARS OLD

Once me neck muscles had developed so I din't
have a floppy head, I became more interesting.
I crapped and pissed meself a lot cos I din't know
what I was doing cos I was a baby. Imagine if
Holly Willoughbooby was yer mam. Feeding
time would've been a totally different experience!

TWO TO FIVE YEARS OLD

I was a little shite. I was naughty cos I din't know right from wrong. I was frustrated cos I cun't talk properly until I was four. My first words were minge and biscuit. But minge weren't a word for a lady's love hole back then, it meant yer face. Anywhere once I started talking I couldn't stop. And that's not all I couldn't stop, I were constantly tugging at me willy. It was me best friend. I fink that's why it's so big today. Yer know like how you talk to plants and they're supposed to grow? Well I din't talk to it but I nurtured it with me hands a lot. And I mean a lot!

FIVE TO TEN YEARS OLD

I grew up pretty fast. Between five and ten, I'd gone through t' playing with toys stage to having a sexually active brain. I was fascinated with women. Loved 'em. I had no control of me willy. It kept going straight. Not fully up, but straight out like it was pointing at girls. I often sat with a cushion on me lap.

TEN TO SIXTEEN YEARS OLD

I'd had many sexual experiences by this stage, including with me teacher Miss Birdmuff who taught me a thing or two about how to pleasure a female. I grew a full complete set of pubes – armpits and knob hairs, and a moustache. I had a constant erection, which I tamed with my seven a day. I was like a walking coat hanger.

I were a breakdancing champion and am still pulling those moves to impress the birds to this day. Must have got the dancing jeans from me dad Billy Ocean.

SIXTEEN TO TWENTY YEARS OLD

By the time I were sixteen, I could totally control
me penis. I owned it, it din't own me, and I liked using
it. I thought I knew everything about t'world. I was
a proper man's end! Had me first holiday with the
lads to Kavos, which led to me first threesome.
Me girlfriend Becky weren't too pleased when she
found out about it but she were getting too clingy.
And I sent her a postcard, what more did she want!

After selling jeans on Leeds market (they were right
good ones – Rhino jeans – really strong in the happy
area), I set up me own business selling Securipoles:
two-foot aluminium shafts to install on your driveway.
They were right tough and protected cars all across
Leeds, and so easy to use that even a woman could use
it. I was crowned Northern Business Man of the Year as
a result and I got to go on Calendar and meet the bang
tidy Carol Vordeman. Shaaaa-ting!

And that is where this book ends, and the first book
Being Keith begins. So go and read that one. If you don't
know what it looks like, here's what it looks like ...

PARENTAL
ADVISORY
EXPLICIT CONTENT

BEING KEITH

*How I Got 'Ere
If You Dont Know How
I Got 'Ere*

LOOKING BACK ⬅▬

As a rule I don't have any regrets. Shit happens, and shit hits the fan, and shit comes out of yer bum and what do I do with it? I flush it away! Oooosh!

I often get asked if I have any advice for the younger generations and If there is one fing me mam taught me that will stay with me forever it is this: Always wear yer wellies if you go paddling – and obviously by wellies she meant rubber jonnies. I've only ever had unprotected sex about twenty-two times but I've been lucky, touch wood. I ain't got wood, I'm sat at a computer writing this! But I've been lucky that anyfing that has touched me wood hasn't given me any STD rings. There may be a few mini Keiths out there but if they come forward I'll go on Jeremy Kylie and do a DMA test and if I am the father I'll do the right ring and send 'em twenty quid a week.

I do wish I had all the knowledge I had now as a kid. But I would've been even more of a cheeky little bastard. Not cocky, just cheeky. It's always strange peoples' perceptions of 'celebrity' (it's getting a bit deep this in't it) people always fink yer minted, but I was doing ok before telly with the Securipoles. I had me own business. But being rich in't about having wedges of coin. It's about happiness I fink. I've always been happy. I fink that's why I look so young cos I've got a positive outlook. Negativity just ages yer. I have a very young and playful nature. Of course I wake up in a bad mood sometimes, just like everyone else, but I'll pump fist, have a shit and a shower, put some mousse in me barnet and scrunch it so it looks like Michael Hutchence, put some stylish clobber on and

I'll fink about what I've got on that day work-wise and I feel overwhelmed with happiness. I never wake up and fink I'm not funny anymore. I don't really set out t' be funny. I set out t'have fun!

T'quote Ferris Bueller: 'Life moves pretty fast. If you don't stop and look around once in a while you could miss it'. I remember the first time I heard that and it stuck with me. That's why I always try and enjoy meself and live in the moment of that enjoyment. Like when yer having it off or copping a feel of some fit bird's boobs. I cherish these moments.

I try to just live in that moment. For everything whether it is a recording *Celebrity Juice*, or *Through t'Keyhole* or what have yer. I always remember Dan the producer of *Juice* (and Holly's husband) asking me before I went on stage, do I ever worry that I'm not gonna be funny ... And I told him, no, cos I don't try be funny. I just do t'job and proper enjoy meself and I fink that's why *Juice* has been a success, cos people enjoy watching us enjoy ourselves.

Sorry I've lost me train of thought. I just popped t'bog t'scrape me hand bag out. I won't eat that again. Oooft! I ate some prawns last night and I fink I got food poisoning from it. Look at me eating prawns! You see, that shows how far I've come! I never thought the day would come when I'd be putting a prawn in me gob, a little pink thing with legs and a pair of black eyes. I must've caught posh. I even buy me bread from M&S. I haven't changed though. And Belly, Pisshole or any of the lads will tell yer that. I still tell fibs about me age, take too long looking in t'mirror, get a bit drunk and cry at girlie films. I love me mum and our Gregory and try t'give back t'people less fortunate than meself,

I'm nice like that. I'm still little Keith Lemon, but I've said it before and I'll say it again, I'm thick as a Coke can.

It could've been a big gamble throwing away what I already had t'come down t' big smoke. But t'quote George McFly, Marty McFly's dad, 'if yer put yer mind to it yer can achieve anything' and I fink that's true.

I was a big fish in a small pond, then a small fish in a big pond, and now I'm riding this telly wave until I fall off. Cos I could do. I could fall of and land right on me bollox.

Right I'll send this t'me publisher, who by the way has the hots for me. Unfortunately for her I'm seeing some fit French bird at the moment. Can't tell what she's talking about but she looks good on all fours.

If I don't see ya through t'week. I'll see ya in me next book.

To be continued ... maybe, we'll see.

All't best,
Big Keith Lemon

little keith lemon

FANKS!

Fanks to all the people that have been nice to me.

Fanks to all me school mates that took part in me life. You know ya names, well ya don't as the names have been changed to protect the innocent.

Fanks t'me mam and dad, and our Greg.

Fanks t'me agent who's fit and me publisher who's also fit. Fanks to everyone at Orion for helping produce this book.

Fanks t'me stylist Heather and me make-up lady Emma. There's a few Emmas I wanna fank actually so fanks to all of them.

Fanks t'all t'people that helped me meck the telly programs I meck. Dan and Leon, Dan and Jamie, Chappers, Arron, both of them! Meriel, erm ...
Joe, Pete, Roy, Paul, James, Ben, Spenny.

Big ups t' Mrs F and the kids! Yeah boi. Fanks for all ya support.

Big ups t'twitter kids, pacifically Ann!

Shout out to everyone at me school, Leeds Market, and Leeds – the whole of Leeds generally.

Fanks t'Keith who's also called Keith and the other Keith (sound man).

Fanks t'all me mates that I hang out with now – the celeb ones and the real ones.

Big ups t'ITV and ITV2 and the other channels that I've been on.

Shout out t'Hooch, adidas and Nandos.

Fanks to everyone who's inspired me but mostly A BIG FANKS TO YOU for buying this book. Ya din't have to but ya did, and I fank you from the bottom of me heart.

If I don't see you though t'week, I'll see you through t'window!

Cheers!

Copyright © Leigh Francis 2014

The right of Leigh Francis to be identified as
the author of this work has been asserted by him in accordance with the
Copyright, Designs and Patents Act 1988.

This edition first published in Great Britain in 2014 by
Orion Books
an imprint of the Orion Publishing Group Ltd
Orion House, 5 Upper St Martin's Lane,
London WC2H 9EA

An Hachette UK Company

1 3 5 7 9 10 8 6 4 2

All rights reserved. Apart from any use permitted under UK copyright law, this
publication may only be reproduced, stored or transmitted, in any form, or by any
means, with prior permission in writing of the publishers or, in the case of
reprographic production, in accordance with the terms of licences issued by the
Copyright Licensing Agency.

A CIP catalogue record for this book is available
from the British Library.

ISBN: 978 1 4091 5247 7

Designer: Smith & Gilmour
Illustrations: Leigh Francis

Picture credits:
Leigh Francis: 4, 10 (right), 11, 14, 17, 19, 23, 25, 33, 34, 35 (centre), 37, 43, 44-5, 48, 57, 61,
64, 70, 76, 77, 87, 93 (top), 97, 101, 105, 111, 112, 119, 131, 135, 143, 149, 150, 151, 159, 171, 175,
184, 189, 195, 203, 204, 207, 209, 222, 224, 235
Andrew Hayes-Watkins: 2, 9, 15, 46, 85, 144, 166, 180-1, 228, 238, 240
Getty: 10 (left), 13, 35 (left and far right), 40, 52, 55, 56, 113, 115, 122, 136, 163, 212, 227,
Rex: 53, 63, 88, 93 (bottom), 95, 99, 121, 169
Shutterstock: 91, 98, 102, 130, 157, 161, 220

Printed in Italy

The Orion Publishing Group's policy is to use papers that are natural, renewable
and recyclable and made from wood grown in sustainable forests. The logging and
manufacturing processes are expected to conform to the environmental
regulations of the country of origin.

Every effort has been made to fulfil requirements with regard to reproducing
copyright material. The author and publisher will be glad to rectify any omissions
at the earliest opportunity.

www.orionbooks.co.uk

Check Out Me Other Books

Suitable for kids (yes, honestly!)

THE BEAVER & THE ELEPHANT

written and drawn by KEITH LEMON

Me Kids Book

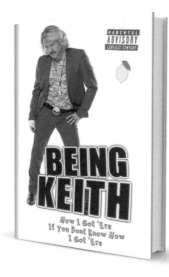

PARENTAL ADVISORY EXPLICIT CONTENT

BEING KEITH

How I Got 'Ere If You Don't Know How I Got 'Ere

'Ere's how I got 'ere

Bang tidy!

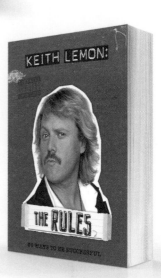

KEITH LEMON: THE RULES

80 WAYS TO BE SUCCESSFUL

Pick up or download your copy today. Ooooosh!